Ana Vázquez

How to Eat Out in Spain

*How to understand the menu
and make yourself understood*

Dictionary and Phrase Book
for the Restaurant

GREMESE

Originally published as:
La Spagna al Ristorante

© 1996 L'Airone Editrice
P.O. Box 14237
00149 Roma - Italy

English translation:
Graham Cole

Jacket design:
Carlo Soldatini

Photocomposition:
IM.A.G.E. - Rome

Printed and bound by:
SO.GRA.TE. - Città di Castello (PG)

© 1997 Gremese International
P.O. Box 14335
00149 Rome - Italy

ISBN 88-7301-097-0

If as we believe, cuisine is part of a country's culture, when visiting Spain it would certainly be a shame to restrict one's interest to its monuments and miss out on an aspect as important as its gastronomic tradition.

It should, however, be remembered that as a result of social, political, and cultural events, Spain did not possess what could rightly be described as a true national cuisine until the beginning of the twentieth century. However, this fact has reinforced the various culinary traditions at a local and regional level, thus avoiding the creation of a false national cuisine for the exclusive use and consumption of foreigners.

Today, every individual region of Spain offers its own local cuisine. Nevertheless, one can also talk of national cuisine, singling out characteristics, products, and ways of cooking which are common to all regions of the peninsula.

In short, being so closely connected with the habits and beliefs of its various socioeconomic classes, Spanish cuisine offers some pleasing surprises and mirrors the complexity of the country's historical events.

The visiting tourist will certainly benefit from having a good basic knowledge of the country's cuisine, as this will enable the most suitable places to be selected and prevent him or her from missing out on the chance to sample the very best dishes that the various regions have to offer. Therefore, the intention of this guide is to provide the foreign tourist with a general overview of Spanish cuisine including a description of its characteristics, typical produce and local specialties, along with indications as to the regions with the best gastronomic traditions. This volume also contains common terms and phrases and the right words for understanding and making oneself understood in the restaurant without difficulty. There is even a section offering a wide range of typical Spanish recipes to try out at home, allowing you to remember and relive the most pleasurable moments of your Spanish holiday.

MAIN CHARACTERISTICS OF SPANISH CUISINE

In order to define the characteristics of Spanish cuisine, it needs to be remembered that there is a wide variety of gastronomic traditions which is due to several different factors. Firstly, we should remember that the country's physical geography has resulted in the natural creation of several distinct regions. For example, the peninsula is bordered by three stretches of water: the Mediterranean Sea, the Atlantic Ocean, and that wonderful fish farm, the coast of the Cantabria province. What is more, Spain has the highest summer temperatures in the whole of Europe (about 40°C, or 100° F, in Cordova and Badajoz), whilst in winter it reaches some extraordinary minimums (20°C or 25°C below zero, or 0° F, in Avila, Soria or Teruel). Finally, historical, cultural and social factors have led to the creation of regions with widely differing ways of life, habits and customs: suffice it to say that there are four official languages!
It therefore follows that the cuisines of these various regions lack common characteristics. However, from a gastronomic point of view it is possible to make a fairly precise distinction between the coastal regions, with a fish-based cuisine, and the inland areas where meat is the predominant ingredient.
Common characteristics of the whole peninsula are the

extremely frequent use of vegetables and pulses, especially in the preparation of starters, and that of spices, such as *pimentón*, red-pepper powder, that can be either mild or hot.

Pork plays an important part in Spanish cuisine and the whole animal is used, from snout to tail, especially when preparing cold cuts and meat-based dishes.

Other important ingredients are fish, shellfish and seafood, the latter being the main ingredient of the famous and highly esteemed *marisco español* that is available the whole year round.

Spain is also particularly rich in cold cuts and cold pork meats, wine and cheese, with an infinite variety available; every region, or rather every district, has its own production.

In conclusion, let us not forget the sweets, cakes and pastries with numerous specialties, usually associated with the traditions of the various religious festivals, to be found both in restaurants and pastry shops.

THE SPANISH MENU

Before describing the classic Spanish menu, it should first be explained that it is common practice in Spain to go to the restaurant and eat *las raciones*. These are a selection of different foods that allow several products to be tasted with just one meal. This dish is extremely common and occurs in almost limitless varieties.

Las tapas are very popular in the Castilian regions and being a smaller-scale version of *las raciones*, are also to be found in bars. Before going home or to the restaurant, it is customary to stop off at no less than two or three bars for a glass of wine, beer or a soft drink: the aperitif is usually served with *las tapas*, delicious appetizers made up of small portions of cooked foods.

Having clarified these points, we are now ready to examine the Spanish menu. It usually consists of three courses: the "first course" that is generally rice or soup with vegetables or pulses, the "main course" that is usually meat or fish often accompanied by salad or potatoes, and a "dessert" that can be fruit, ice cream or a local sweet.

The meal will be rounded off with coffee and a local liqueur.

SPANISH RESTAURANTS

When eating out in Spain, there is certainly no shortage of choice and at prices to suit all pockets. Nearly all the hotels have their own restaurant, and while quality may differ from one to another, the overall standard is generally more than acceptable.

In any event, however, the best way of getting to know Spanish cuisine is to go to a proper restaurant where typical local dishes are more readily available which can rightly be considered "the genuine article."

In addition to the restaurants, there are the *bodegas*, a kind of tavern, which specialize in *las raciones* and allow one to sample a bit of everything at very reasonable prices. Fortunately, we may rest assured that be it hotel, tavern, large or small restaurant, the food is never disappointing. We can add, however, that the restaurants and taverns at some distance from the main streets, and perhaps hidden away in the back streets of the old town, are well worth discovering. A good rule of thumb to finding the best area for eating out: every Spanish city has a square called "Plaza Mayor" situated in its oldest part, and it is there that the best local restaurants are to be found with the guarantee of a sumptuous, genuine cuisine.

Whilst not strictly necessary, it is advisable to book, especially on Saturdays and Sunday lunchtime.

In any event, before making a definite decision, it is well worth consulting the price list that can be found on display at the entrance to most restaurants and other eating houses. Besides offering a hint as to prices, it will also give some idea as to the type of food served.

When the bill arrives, you will usually have the opportunity of paying with one of the major credit cards, especially in cities and tourist resorts.

Prices vary according to one's chosen venue. Average cost of a full meal with drinks is around 2,500-3,000 pesetas per head. It is clear that a menu offering fresh fish will be more expensive and it is then advisable to choose somewhere in the vicinity of the port where good value for money will be offered.

Whether in bar, tavern or restaurant, the bill includes VAT or other local taxes, service and cover charge. It is customary to leave the waiter a tip in proportion to the total amount of the bill.

Typical opening hours are from noon to 3.30 P.M. for lunch and from 7.00 P.M. until late for dinner. However, many eating places are open all day.

CHEESES

Spain boasts a wide variety of cheeses with production concentrated above all in the north of the peninsula.

The following is a description of each of the most common cheeses along with its region of origin. The list is by no means exhaustive since hundreds of different types exist. As in the case of other products, it is a good idea to seek the waiter's advice if wishing to sample the best local specialties.

Afuega'l pitu: Asturias. In *bable* (Asturian) dialect it literally means "drown the chick" which is due to its consistency: it is so dry that it is often eaten with honey to assist swallowing. Originally mild and white, a variety exists containing added *pimentón* which gives it a strong flavor and pink coloring.

Alicante: Alicante. Medium-fat cheese made with goat's milk. It is soft and white. Smells and tastes of cow's milk. It is not left to mature and should be eaten whilst fresh.

Armada: Castile-León. Also known as *calostro* or *sobado*, it is the only known cheese produced with cow's colostrum, from second or third milking (up to the fifth). Fat content is 44%. It is prism-shaped with rounded edges. The rind is medium hard and white without holes. The cheese itself has a medium-hard consistency. Flavor is strong and slightly bitter. Keeps for up to 3 years.

Burgos: Castile-León. This full-fat soft cheese is made from sheep's milk. It is not left to mature and should be eaten straight away. White and cylinder-shaped, it has a mild taste and a distinctive fragrance. Will not keep for more than 48 hours.

Cabrales: Asturias. A mixture of cow's, sheep's and goat's milk. The most prized variety is obtained by using the rennet of kids or lambs which have been slaughtered immediately after suckling and before the milk has been digested. The greenish color is due to a particular mold which develops whilst the cheese is left to mature in caves. The whole cheeses are covered with animal droppings as tradition requires. Once the cheese has reached the right degree of greasiness, it is wrapped in maple leaves and is then ready for sale. It has an intense smell and a fairly strong flavor.

Cerebro: Galicia. A half-fat cheese made from cow's milk with a mushroom shape. The rind is white and medium hard with cracks. The cheese itself is medium hard, white, and has a fairly bitter flavor. It is usually eaten fresh, but can be kept for up to six months.

Gamonedo: Asturias. Also known as *gamoneu*. This medium-fat cheese is similar to *cabrales* but is left to mature for a shorter period and in different conditions. This means that the mold does not have the same effect and the cheese obtained contains less fat. A further difference is that it is not wrapped in maple leaves.

Gorbea: Basque Country. It is obtained by using sheep's milk and has a fat content of 45%. The rind is yellow, hard and smooth. The cheese itself is slightly yellow and of firm consistency with holes. Strong smell and flavor. It is left to mature for a month and will keep for between 1 and 2 years.

Idiazábal: Basque Country. Other names are *urbia*, *aralar* and *urbasa*. A full-fat cheese made from sheep's milk, it is smoked and has a very particular smell. The rind is smooth whilst the cheese itself is yellow in color. It is left to mature for a month and will keep for one year.

León: Castile-León. Full-fat cheese obtained from cow's milk. It contains a great deal of salt. The cheese itself is white, medium-hard and strong-flavored.

Orduña: Basque Country. Full-fat cheese obtained from sheep's milk. It has a hard, yellowish rind and a sharp flavor.

Pasiego prensado: Cantabria. Made from whole cow's milk, this is a soft cheese with a white, smooth crust. It is mild-tasting and smells of fresh cream. Prepared in only a few days, it can be kept for months.

Pasiego sin prensar: Cantabria. It is a full-fat cheese made from whole cow's milk, although sheep's milk is sometimes added. The cheese itself is soft with a mildish flavor and the smell of milk. It is a fresh cheese which will keep for no more than a week.

Picón de Treviso: Cantabria. A full-fat cheese which is very similar to *cabrales*. Usually made from whole cow's milk, although goat's and sheep's milk are sometimes used. The rind is gray and is covered with the leaves of several different trees. The cheese itself is medium hard and has a yellowish-white and blue coloring. Intense aroma and very sharp flavor. It is left to mature for 6 months.

Puzol: Valencia. Full-fat cheese made from sheep's milk. It is soft, white and rindless. It is not left to mature and should be consumed within 24 to 48 hours.

Queso de los Beyos: Asturias. Also known as *beyusco*, it is a hard cheese made from sheep's or goat's milk, or sometimes both. In recent years the tendency to use cow's milk has developed. It is a full-fat, mature, slightly-smoked cheese.

Quesucos de Lebeña: Cantabria. It is also called *quesines* or *quesucos de Avila*. It is a medium-hard, smoked cheese made from cow's, goat's and sheep's milk (or sometimes just cow's milk). Fat content is fairly high. The cheese itself has a firm consistency, yellowish color and a distinctive smell. Will keep for only a short time.

San Simón: Galicia. It is prepared using whole cow's milk and has a fat content of 26%. It is pear-shaped. The rind is smoked, hard and white. The cheese itself has a firm consistency and is creamy with a slightly bitter taste. It is left to mature for a month and will keep for up to 2 years.

Soria: Castile-León. Full-fat, fresh cheese made from goat's milk. It is white with a salty flavor.

Tetilla: Galicia. It is prepared using whole cow's milk and has a fat content of 40%. It is white, pie-shaped and rindless. It has a distinctive smell and a very pleasant taste that is slightly salty and bitter.

Ulloa: Galicia. Also known as *gallego*, *patela* and *perilla*. It is made from cow's milk and has a fat content of 45%. It is either pie-shaped or in the form of a flat cylinder. The cheese itself is soft and white, whilst the rind is yellowish with a certain elasticity.

Valdeteja: Castile-León. Cheese with an elevated fat content made from whole goat's milk. The rind is smooth, dry, medium hard and yellowish in color. Flavor is sharp.

Villalón: Castile-León. Also known as *pata de mulo*, it is made from sheep's milk. It is a fresh, full-fat cheese similar to *burgos* (see above). It is soft, white and rindless.

Cold cut meats are products typical of Spanish gastronomic culture. You will find them all over the peninsula in abundant supply and with thousands of different shapes and flavors. They can be placed into different groups according to the method of preparation and the ingredients used: a distinction can be made between smoked products (the north of Spain), those with spices (all over the Mediterranean zone), those with *pimentón* – powdered red pepper similar to paprika – and lastly those with garlic (in Andalusia and Estremadura). We should also add to this list products made from game which are commonly found all over Spain, and those from the Canary Islands that have special characteristics.

Andoya: Asturias. A smoked cold cut meat made using loin meats. *Xuan* is a variety containing added cow- and pig-tongue.

Blancos: Castile-La Mancha. Pork cold cuts prepared with lard, lean meat and bacon chopped into pieces and mixed with eggs and spices such as white and black pepper, nutmeg, etc. The presence of the eggs makes them highly perishable and for this reason they must be consumed immediately.

Blanquet: Balearic Islands/Catalonia/Valencia. Another pork cold cut meat made using lard, lean cuts, bacon and the head of the pig. These are mixed with white pepper, cinnamon, cloves, nutmeg, pine nuts and salt. May be eaten raw, roasted or fried.

Botelo: Galicia. A smoked cold cut meat, prepared from small pieces of rib, vertebra and other bones along with their muscular tissue. Added to the meat are pig's lard, garlic, the famous *pimentón* (both mild and hot varieties), and oregano. It is eaten boiled.

Butifarra: Catalonia/Valencia/Murcia/Balearic Islands. This cold cut meat is typical of the entire eastern zone of the peninsula. Its ingredients are lean cuts of pork, bacon and lard, and just one spice: pepper. Nevertheless, its method of preparation can vary from region to region, with the addition of other ingredients such as rice, liver, onion, etc.

Cecina: Castile-León. Similar to ham but prepared from the lower part of the leg of pork. There exists a variety of *cecina* which uses billy goat instead of pork.

Chistorra: Navarra. Classic local cold cut meat made from pork and beef with bacon and lard. Spice is provided by the ever-present *pimentón*. It can be eaten roasted, grilled or fried.

Chorizo: the whole of Spain. The typical Spanish salami prepared from lean cuts of pork and lard. Its characteristic red color is due to the added *pimentón*. There are an infinite number of varieties as it is produced all over the peninsula and on the islands.

Fariñón: Asturias. One of the main characteristics of this cold cut meat is the presence of corn meal amongst the ingredients. The others are lean pork, lard and pig's blood, whilst the spices are comprised of oregano, bay leaf and *pimentón*.

Fuet: Catalonia. Typical local salami whose ingredients are lean pork and rindless bacon spiced with white pepper. It is also produced using belly of spring lamb with the notable addition of sugar.

Jamon: the whole of Spain. This is the famous Spanish ham which like *chorizo* is produced in virtually every Spanish region.

Lacón: Galicia. This cold cut meat is prepared using shoulder of pork. The bone is removed and salt is added to the meat. This is certainly one of the most typical of the region of Galicia.

Lomo embuchado: Castile/Andalusia/Estremadura/Aragón. This cold cut meat is prepared from fatless loin of pork. Main spices used are *pimentón* and oregano. It is eaten raw.

Longaniza: the entire peninsula. Very similar to *chorizo* since it contains the same meat. However, the spices and tripe used differ from region to region.

Morcilla: the whole of Spain. The basic ingredients are always the same: lard, fat, pig's blood and above all, onion. Regional variations may result from the addition of other ingredients such as rice, sugar, egg, etc. However, it is usually cooked in the same way: boiled.

Morcón: Estremadura/Andalusia/Valencia. This cold cut meat is typical of the southern peninsula and its ingredients are lean cuts of pork and pig's head, salt, pepper, *pimentón* and garlic. In some areas, white wine is added. It is eaten raw.

Salchicha: Estremadura/Castile. Lean meat, fresh lard, white pepper, oregano and mild *pimentón* are the basic ingredients of this type of cold cut meat. The added spices are subject to variation: one may find nutmeg, cloves, garlic, cinnamon, etc.

Salchichón: central regions. This is almost identical to *chorizo*, the one difference being the absence of *pimentón*.

Sobrasada: Aragón/Alicante/Catalonia/Balearic Islands. It is made using lean pork and pig's lard with the addition of *pimentón*. Once preparation is complete, a sauce is obtained which is smooth and of equal consistency: it is eaten spread over bread.

Torteta: Catalonia/Aragón. This popular product is of dark appearance with a mild flavor. Its ingredients are pig's blood and cinnamon. It is usually eaten fried or roasted.

Los mariscos (shellfish and other seafood) are a very important part of Spanish gastronomic culture, especially in the peninsula's northern regions, since the Cantabrian coast is the main source of shellfish and other crustaceans. It is therefore fitting that an entire section be dedicated to these most excellent dishes that are normally eaten boiled or grilled without losing their natural flavor. Tradition wants that the best months for *mariscos* are those containing the letter "R"; therefore, they are best avoided in May, June, July and August.

Almeja: clams are one of the most popular shellfish due to their characteristic delicate flavor. From a gastronomic point of view, the methods of preparation are numerous: from simple steaming to more sophisticated recipes, without forgetting that they are also eaten raw with a sprinkling of lemon.

Berberecho: a shellfish with a semicircular shell, smaller than the clam but no less tasty. Can be eaten in many ways including raw, with lemon, fried, boiled, etc.

Bígaro: a small rock snail, it is boiled and usually eaten as a starter.

Buey de mar: crustacean which is the largest member of the crab family. Despite its size, it is somewhat lacking in flesh. The claws are the tastiest part, whilst liver and roe are also quite delicious.

Cangrejo de mar: This sea crab is one of the most popular. Its meat is quite exquisite but is difficult to extract.

Centollo: is the king of Spanish shellfish; a species of spider crab, it is eaten boiled with a pinch of salt and a bay leaf.

Cigala: the quality of this species of scampi depends on the temperature of the sea: the colder the water where it lives, the more choice is its meat.

Chirla: is a shellfish related to the clam but of smaller dimensions. For this reason it commands a lower price and is therefore often used as a substitute.

Gamba: prawns are one of the most popular shellfish of the coastal regions, especially in bars that serve the famous *tapas*. Methods of preparation include grilled, boiled, with garlic, etc.

Langosta: if the king of the crustaceans is the centollo, the queen has to be the lobster. The cooking point needs to be just right, not over or undercooked, in order to fully appreciate the flavor and smell of the sea: in this case its taste is really worth savoring. The tastiest, and most sought after variety is the *bogayante* that can be identified by its blue shell and larger claws.

Langostino: it is a species of baby lobster found in Mediterranean waters and also on the northern coast.

Mejillón: mussels. Known as the poor man's *el marisco*, but one could certainly say "blessed are the poor"... mussels are excellent food, having both a high nutritional value (they are very rich in proteins, calories and fats) and an exquisite flavor. Methods of preparation are numerous: boiled, steamed, with lemon, with spicy sauces, etc.

Nécora: is a variety of *cangrejo de mar* (see above) and some will say that it is the best seafood there is. A peculiarity of this crustacean is the fifth pair of claws which are oar-shaped. Eaten in all regions.

Ostra: the queen of shellfish. Whether raw or boiled, oysters are always to be found in the best restaurants, although they are most closely associated with the Christmas period. Spanish oysters are considered amongst the most delicious in the whole world.

Percebe: although a crustacean, the barnacle could easily be mistaken for a shellfish. It is divided into two parts: the shell and the stalk, and it is the latter part that is edible. Boiled and served immediately, it is yet another seafood delicacy that is well worth trying even though it is somewhat expensive. The smaller examples of this crustacean are the tastiest ones.

Vieira: these shellfish are amongst the tastiest on offer with abundant meat. This allows thousands of different dishes to be prepared, although they are also excellent eaten raw.

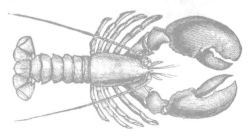

Every region of Spain has its own recipes for local homemade sweets. Many restaurants and other eating places offer delicious homemade desserts prepared to a traditional recipe.

The infinite variety of Spanish sweets makes it impossible to list them all. We therefore propose a select list of the better-known ones that you will find in restaurants and pastry shops throughout the country.

Almendras garrapiñadas: almonds and sugar are placed in a saucepan and heated until the sugar turns to caramel and forms a coating over the almonds.

Arroz con leche: a kind of risotto cooked in milk and flavored with butter, sugar, cinnamon and egg.

Bizcochos: small round cakes consisting of sponge cake soaked in rum.

Brazo de gitano: Cylindrical, like a Swiss roll, it consists of sponge cake soaked in syrup, filled with custard and covered in meringue.

Buñuelos: fritters of flour, eggs, sugar, butter, lemon and brandy; they are fried and covered in sugar.

Crema catalana; as the name suggests, it is a sweet typical of Catalonia. It consists of a cream made from sugar, milk, eggs and lemon which is then covered with a layer of caramel.

Churros: although these sweets are a specialty of Madrid, they are nowadays found all over the country. The mixture consisting of flour, water and salt is divided into portions vaguely resembling a tube: these are then fried and sprinkled with sugar. They are traditionally eaten on New Year's Day with a nice cup of hot chocolate.

Ensaimada: spiral-shaped pastry filled with cream. A typical specialty of Catalonia and the Balearic Islands, it is by now a common sight in almost every Spanish pastry shop.

Flan: a pudding with a thousand possible flavors including chocolate, orange, coffee, lemon, etc. It is prepared with both egg and vanilla.

Helados: the best Spanish ice cream is to be found above all in coastal areas, without doubt for climatic reasons. Nevertheless, it can also be found in other regions and once again in an infinite number of flavors.

Lenguas de gato: pastries prepared with simple ingredients – flour, eggs, sugar, butter – but with a distinctive tongue shape as suggested by the name itself, which literally means "cat's tongue".

Manzanas al horno: oven-baked apples with a part removed to enable orange juice, yoghurt and sultanas to be added.

Natillas: similar to a flan, vanilla flavored.

Pastel de la abuela: a kind of tart containing apricot jam.

Polvorones: a sweet with a slight hint of cinnamon. It is noted for the fact that it melts in the mouth. Usually eaten at Christmas.

Tocinillos: a kind of pudding that is very sweet and of rich consistency.

Torrijas: this is nothing more than slices of bread soaked in milk and then egg. They are then fried in a frying pan and finally left to cook in wine along with some sugar.

Yemas: sweets prepared with egg yolks. Various flavors exist including lemon, orange, etc. They are somewhat jelly-like.

Spain is a country renowned for its wines. Hundreds of types are produced, from whites to rosés, and reds to liqueur-like dessert wines. Every region boasts its own special type. Castile is noted for its red wines, such as Cava di Catalogna, whilst Andalusia is famous for Jerez. As an entire book could be written on the subject, we shall restrict our list to the better-known wines and their places of origin.

Albariño: Galicia. A very particular white wine famous throughout Spain. It has a bitter taste and is excellent served with *los mariscos*.

Alcublas: Valencia. White wine with a slight hint of almond. It is between 10° and 13° proof.

Betanzos: Castile-León. A red wine, light in both body and color, with a bitter flavor.

Bierzo: Castile-León. White, red and rosé varieties exist. It is flavored with fruit and is between 10° and 11° proof.

Cava: Catalonia. Many varieties exist but it is always sparkling white and served chilled.

Cheste: Valencia. Dry white table wine, 15° proof.

Chulilla: Valencia. Red dessert wine, 13° proof.

Haro: Murcia. Light red wine, slightly bitter but very refreshing.

Jerez: Andalusia. A typical wine of the region. There are many types, but they are always white, quite dry wines with a high alcoholic contert. Must be served very cold.

Jumilla monastrel: Murcia. Very aromatic wine with a cherry-red color, 15° proof.

Jumilla seco: Murcia. Red table wine with the same alcoholic strength as the *monastrel*.

Los Oteros: Castile-León. Light red wine between 10° and 13° proof.

Monterrey: Galicia. Both red and white varieties exist. Both have a high alcoholic content and whilst not particularly bitter, neither has much of a fragrance.

Montilla: Andalusia. Similar to *Jerez*, but more bitter with a slight hint of almond.

Montroy: Valencia. Sweet Muscat dessert wine.

Ribeiro: Galicia. Typical local wine. It is not drunk from a wine glass, but a small kind of cup is used. It has a pleasant taste and is 13° proof.

Rosal: Galicia. A cheerful white wine flavored with fruit.

Rueda: Castile-León. A red aged wine, 15° proof.

Toro: Castile-León. A dark full-bodied red wine. It is flavored with fruit and has a high alcoholic content.

Valdeorras: Galicia. Clear dry white wine, 12° proof.

Valdevimbre: Castile-León. A light fragrant red wine flavored with fruit.

There are some other typical local products in Spain that do not fall into the categories previously covered, but are certainly worth trying or even buying to take back home. Once again, our list is not exhaustive and only includes the more important products.

Canapés: small triangular slices of bread garnished with a variety of different sauces. Commonly served in the more sumptuous restaurants as hors-d'oeuvres.

Empanada: it is a savory pie with puff pastry or dough that may be filled with various ingredients. The most common fillings are tuna or minced meat with tomato sauce and onion. Typical dish of the regions of Galicia and Asturias, it is now commonly found throughout the whole country.

Empanadilla: a kind of savory pancake that contains the same ingredients as *empanada* and is fried.

Migas: cubes of bread that are fried and eaten along with the traditional Spanish purée.

Sangría: this is one of the most famous Spanish drinks and originates from the southern central region. It is a cocktail obtained by mixing red wine, Jerez, orangeade, sugar and slices of fruit (apple, pear, orange and lemon). It is usually served chilled.

Sidra: Asturias. Typical of this region, it is the end result of the complete or partial fermentation of apple juice. It has a bitter taste and is 6° proof. It is drunk from a special wide glass and is poured as follows: the bottle is taken in the right hand and placed above one's head; the glass is held in the left hand at waist height, at which point a quantity of cider equal to 180 cc is poured. This is known as "culin" and is drunk in one single mouthful. Everyone drinks from the same glass.

Torta: a sweet flat cake covered in sugar that is to be found in food stores and cakeshops.

Albóndigas: small balls of minced meat that are fried and then cooked in a thousand different ways.

Bechamel: creamy sauce prepared with milk, flour and butter. It is used above all for oven-cooked dishes. Pieces of chicken or veal are added to the sauce to make Spanish croquettes (very rarely are they made with potato).

Escalopes: breaded minute steaks.

Filete: any type of fried minute steak.

Puré: mashed potatoes served along with the meat, but also as a starter to which vegetables are added. In the latter case its consistency is a lot more liquid.

Rollos: roulades of meat with filling; they come in various sizes with the smaller type known as *niños envueltos.*

Even though the dishes described in this chapter have different regional origins, today they are commonly found throughout the country and are now firmly established as part of Spain's gastronomic heritage.

This does not necessarily mean that some dishes are better in their respective zones of provenance. It is worth giving them a try even when cooked to a recipe which does not follow the original to the letter.

The dishes mentioned below are listed in alphabetical order according to their Spanish name and an indication as to where you will find them on the menu.

Alcachofas rellenas (Stuffed artichokes): side dish. Fried artichokes with a filling of ham and bread that is also fried.

Almejas a la marinera (Clam marinade): starter or *ración*. A plate of clams cooked with carrot, leek, lemon, garlic, parsley and flour.

Almejas guisadas (Clams): starter or *ración*. A plate of clams cooked with abundant onion.

Anguilas al horno (Baked eel): main course. The eel is first cooked with abundant onion and then put in the oven.

Anguilas con guisantes (Eel and peas) main course. In this case the eel is cooked with onion, peas and *pimentón* but is not placed in the oven as baked eel. (See above).

Arroz blanco (White rice): starter or sometimes all-in-one dish. Boiled rice with fried tomatoes and sometimes also fried egg.

Arroz con almejas (Rice and clams): starter. The clams are first cooked along with onion, then added to the rice, and finally mixed together in a frying pan.

Arroz con riñones (Rice and kidneys): starter. Identical in all respects to the previous dish apart from the addition of kidneys.

Atún asado (Baked tuna): main course. The fish is cooked with abundant onion and served with a side dish of potatoes.

Atún con tomate (Tuna and tomato): main course. Similar to the previous dish but cooked in a tomato sauce. Sometimes bell peppers may be added.

Bacalao al horno (Baked dried salted cod): main course. The fish is prepared with a little tomato, parsley and white wine. There are, in fact, many other dishes which have dried salted cod as the main ingredient and these are covered in the section, "Regional Dishes." It is a commonly used fish in the restaurants of northern Spain, although it can now be found all over the country.

Besugo al horno (Baked sea bream): main course. The fish is baked in the oven with potatoes and onion.

Cabrito asado (Roast kid goat): main course. This dish is typical of the central regions of the peninsula. The meat is cooked in the oven with a few potatoes.

Calamares a la romana (Deep-fried squid): *ración*. Deep-fried squid rings with a sprinkling of lemon.

Calamares en su tinta (Squid): main course. The squid are cooked in their own black ink sauce with abundant onion and a little ham.

Callos (Tripe): *ración*. Famous throughout Spain, this dish is extremely spicy due to the fact that the tripe is cooked along with abundant chili pepper and *pimentón*.

Canelones (Cannelloni): all-in-one dish. This dish was of course imported from Italy, but is by now commonly found throughout Spain.

Carne mechada: main course. A cut of veal similar to that often used for pot roasts: the meat is larded (small cuts are made into which pieces of lard are inserted) although bell peppers, carrots, etc. are also added. It is cooked in its juices and then cut into thin slices for serving.

Cocido madrileño: all-in-one dish. Whilst its origins can be traced to Madrid, as its name would indicate, it is in fact one of the hallmarks of Spanish cuisine. It effectively consists of two courses. Firstly chick-peas, pork, salami and savoy cabbage are cooked together; the resulting broth is served with pasta, as a soup, and makes up the first course. The second course follows, consisting of the chick-peas, meat and vegetables. This is a somewhat heavy dish that is best suited to the winter months.

Cochinillo asado: main course. Oven-roasted suckling pig. A typical dish of the Castile region, it can now be found in many Spanish restaurants. In the local Castilian restaurants, it is cut with a plate rather than a knife in order to show how tender it is.

Codorniz en su salsa (Quail): main course. The quail are cooked with onion, white wine and a little flour.

Coliflor frita (Fried cauliflower): starter. The cauliflower is first chopped into small pieces, then boiled in salted water, and finally covered in flour and fried. Afterwards it is cooked with a little white wine and tomato.

Compota de manzana: dessert. Apples cooked with lemon and sugar. Pears may also be used.

Conejo (Rabbit): main course. The rabbit is cut into small pieces and cooked with a little onion, mushroom and white wine.

Congrio con almejas (Conger eel and clam): main course or all-in-one dish. Delicious. The eel is cooked in slices together with the clams, a little onion, and white wine.

Chanfaina: *ración*. A rather particular dish that is prepared with the parts of the pig of less common usage: heart, lung, blood, and abundant *pimentón*.

Chipirones fritos: main course. Small whole squid, stuffed with their own tentacles, coated in flour, and then fried until golden and crunchy.

Chuletas/Chuletillas de cordero (Spring-lamb cutlets): main course. The cutlets may be grilled or cooked in a frying pan and are served with a salad or French fries.

Chuletón (Giant steak): main course. A very large steak that can weigh more than 2 pounds (1 kilo) grilled and served with a salad or French fries.

Embutidos mixtos: hors-d'oeuvre. A selection of appetizers with ham, salami and different cheeses.

Ensaladilla rusa (Russian salad): starter. Usually eaten during the summer months, it is a mixture of potatoes, sliced carrots, peas, tuna, hard-boiled eggs, and mayonnaise.

Entrecote de ternera: main course. Roast veal with potatoes or vegetables.

Espárragos (Asparagus): *ración*. The asparagus is boiled and eaten as it is, or with a little mayonnaise.

Filetes de ternera (Veal minute steaks): main course. The steaks are cooked in the frying pan, usually with garlic, and are served with a salad or French fries.

Filetes empanados (Breaded minute steaks): main course. The minute steaks are usually served with fried peppers or potatoes.

Gratinado de berenjenas (Eggplant au gratin): side dish. Sliced eggplant covered in grated cheese and cooked in the oven until a light crust is formed.

Huevos al plato (Egg platter): main course. The eggs are served in the same casserole dish in which they are cooked along with a mixture of peas, ham and peppers.

Jamón con guisantes (Ham and peas): main course. Small pieces of ham and peas cooked with onion and white wine.

Judías verdes (French beans): starter. The beans are first boiled and then cooked with a little tomato and potatoes.

Langostinos (Baby lobsters): *ración*. They may be grilled or boiled. In the latter case they are served with a sprinkling of lemon.

Lenguado al horno (Baked sole): main course. The fish is baked in the oven and served with potatoes.

Lubina asada (Sea bass): main course. Oven-baked bass with pepper, lemon and parsley.

Manzanas rellenas de nuez y coco (dessert): after scooping out the center of the apples and removing the core, they are filled with a mixture of sugar, walnuts, and coconut and "sealed off" with butter. The apples are then sprinkled with Jerez and baked in the oven.

Mejillones al vapor (Steamed mussels): *ración*. The steaming brings out the full flavor of the mussels and they merely require a squeeze of lemon before serving.

Menestra (Soup): starter. A minestrone of mixed vegetables and small pieces of pork or veal, it is usually eaten in the winter months.

Merluza a la cazuela (Hake): the fish is cooked together with clams, asparagus, and peppers. It is served in the same casserole dish in which it is cooked.

Milhojas (Millefeuille or Napoleon): dessert. A rich confection of puff pastry split and filled with cream and meringue.

Morcilla: *ración*. The main ingredient is black pudding either fried or boiled; in both cases abundant *pimentón* is added. This fairly spicy dish is typically found in all Spanish regions and is well worth trying.

Nata con nueces (Walnuts and cream): dessert. A specialty of the Mediterranean regions. The shelled walnuts are served in a sundae dish along with the cream.

Paella: all-in-one dish. This is certainly the best known dish of all as regards Spanish cuisine and originates from Valencia. It is a risotto containing pork and chicken, peppers, mussels and clams, a little tomato, peas, and saffron for coloring. However, there are a thousand, local variations of this recipe. It may be prepared exclusively with meat or just fish, but in any event it is worth trying.

Patatas con carne (Meat and potatoes): all-in-one dish. A dish of rice, veal and potatoes. There is another recipe that uses prawns, but the main spice is always *pimentón*.

Pato al horno (Roast duck): main course. The duck is oven-roasted along with the potatoes.

Pechugas de pollo (Chicken breast): main course. The chicken breasts are first fried and then placed in a casserole dish and cooked with a few peppers, tomato and onion.

Picadillo: *ración*. This dish is prepared with the ingredients used for a normal salami, but instead of being stuffed into the skin, the mixture is fried.

Pimientos rellenos: *ración*. Dish made with stuffed bell peppers baked in the oven.

Pincho moruno: main course. Grilled pork kebabs, with pieces of sausage and peppers spiced with hot *pimentón*.

Pollo asado (Roast chicken): main course. Oven-roasted chicken and potatoes.

Pulpo a la gallega (Octopus): main course. The octopus is boiled with potatoes and then cut into not very large pieces. It is seasoned with a little oil and spicy *pimentón*.

Revuelto de gambas y ajetes: *ración*. Scrambled eggs with fried prawns and garlic.

Rollos de tenera (Veal roulades): main course. Classic dish of veal roulades cooked in an earthenware casserole dish with a few vegetables.

Salmón asado (Baked salmon): main course. The fish is cooked in the oven and served with a few potatoes or a salad.

Sardinas fritas (Fried sardines): *ración*. Typically found in the northern regions where it is a firm favorite amongst the local inhabitants.

Solomillo: main course. Sliced or whole joint of pork cooked with carrots, peppers and other vegetables.

Sopa de ajo: starter. A simple soup of water, bread, garlic and *pimentón*. Similar to the bread soup of certain Italian regions, it is traditionally eaten on New Year's Eve.

Sopa de puré: starter. A fairly liquid purée of vegetables, pulses and sometimes meat.

Sorbete de naranja: (Orange sherbet): dessert. Made with oranges, it is a bit like ice cream but with a less creamy consistency.

Suflé de patatas: main course. A timbale (or kind of flan) of potatoes with layers of vegetables and minced meat (usually veal).

Tortilla española (Spanish omelette): *ración* or main course. A potato and onion omelette. Very simple but quite excellent. A dish worth ordering in the restaurant or trying out at home.

Tortilla francesa (French omelette): main course. A plain egg omelette. If asparagus is added, the name is *tortilla de esparragos,* with cheese *tortilla de queso*, etc.

Tortilla de ropa vieja (Leftovers omelette): main course. Like the *tortilla española* but with the addition of the previous day's leftovers: meat, vegetables, pulses... anything goes.

Tortilla paisana (Country omelette): main course. Like the *tortilla española* but with added potatoes and vegetables such as zucchini, bell peppers, etc.

Truchas al horno (Baked trout); main course. Oven-cooked trout stuffed with ham.

Truchas escabechadas (Trout in vinegar): main course. Instead of using oil, the trout are marinated in vinegar.

Listing the infinite variety of regional specialties would take up far more space than we have available. In the circumstances, we shall restrict our list to the more common local dishes which are typically found in each region. As a brief introduction to this section, a description of the main characteristics of each region's cuisine is offered.

The layout is the same as for "National Dishes" with an indication as to the position of the dish on the menu along with its main ingredients.

ANDALUSIA

Andalusian cuisine has always been considered poor, primitive and meager. The region's gastronomic tradition is restricted to just a few specialties, such as the famous *gazpacho andaluz*.

However, it should not be forgotten that in Andalusia eggs are a very important ingredient and are used in a wide variety of ways: scrambled, fried, etc. An important place is also held by the region's vegetables and small fried fish. Bull's meat is typical of the area, but veal and beef are also widely used.

Ham is a major ingredient of Andalusian cuisine.

Abajá de Algeciras: starter. A kind of soup consisting of fish stock with white wine. The fish is served afterwards as a second course.

Chanfaína: main course. Stewed chicken served in a sauce of onion, bell peppers, almonds, nutmeg.

REGIONAL DISHES

Gazpacho andulaz: all-in-one dish. A cold soup of raw vegetables prepared with tomato, cucumber, bread, garlic, bell peppers, oil, salt, and vinegar; the ingredients are finely chopped and served chilled.

Guiso de caracoles: main course. Stewed snails with small pieces of Sierra ham, tomatoes, bell peppers, garlic, almonds, and pine nuts.

Guiso de rabo de toro: main course. A stew of bull's tail cooked with tomato, onion and pepper. The ingredients are soaked in *Montilla* which is a local wine.

Huevos a la flamenca: main course. Fried eggs served with a sauce of peas, ham, tomato, and beans.

Olla gitana: side dish. Plate of mixed vegetables, French beans, potatoes, bell peppers, tomatoes with chick-peas, pears, and almonds, seasoned with vinegar, oil and mild paprika.

Pollo al Jerez: main course. Chicken cooked in Jerez wine with mushrooms and onions.

Riñones al Jerez: main course. Kidney and onion cooked in the region's local Jerez wine.

ASTURIAS AND CANTABRIA

We have decided to cover these two regions together since they encompass a single culinary zone, even though they are completely different from a historical, political, and social point of view.

Gastronomically speaking, Asturias is best known for its *fabada asturiana*; the zone is rich in fish, meat, and sliced ham and salami.

Cantabria enjoys an extremely varied, fish-based cuisine, although it is also rich in cheeses; butter is typically found in the rice-based dishes.

Angulas a la cazuela: main course. Eel fry cooked with garlic, oil, and chili pepper in small earthenware pans.

Caldereta asturiana: all-in-one dish: A mixture of small cuts of fish, mussels, clams, prawns, *centollo*, lobster, scampi, and limpets, cooked with wine, nutmeg, chili pepper, *pimentón*, onion, bell peppers, lemon, garlic, and parsley.

Estofado a la asturiana: main course. Beef stew cooked in lard with abundant vegetables and various herbs and spices.

Estofado de buey (Beef stew): main course. Dish prepared with leg of ox, but also with beef and vegetables. The dish is served with the meat in the center surrounded by the vegetables.

Fabada asturiana: starter. A somewhat heavy dish consisting of beans, *lacón*, lard, *morcilla*, onion, and salami.

Fabes con almejes: main course. Mixed dish of clam marinade, mussels, and beans, seasoned with parsley, bay leaf, onion, garlic, and saffron with a sprinkling of breadcrumbs.

Frixuelos: dessert. A kind of flapjack made with flour, egg, sugar, aniseed, salt, and oil.

Merluza a la sidra (Cidered hake): main course. Cooked in the oven, the hake is covered in a sauce of potatoes, tomatoes, and abundant cider.

Morros de ternera a la asturiana: main course. Spicy stew of snout and leg of veal, diced ham, onion, garlic, and walnuts.

Pollo campurriano: main course. Chicken chopped into pieces with rice and vegetables. A fairly heavy dish in that it contains abundant onion and lard.

BALEARIC ISLANDS

The islands offer a rich variety of cuisine. Typical are the soups and pork, the latter being used in the excellent *sobrasada*.

Burrida de ratjada: main course. Skate stewed in an almond sauce.

Caldereta de langosta: all-in-one dish. Pieces of lobster with green bell peppers, eggs, and tomatoes.

Caracoles pagesos: main course. Snails cooked in wine and vinegar with herbs and spices.

Carne de cerdo con leche: main course. Pork cooked in milk with garlic and mild paprika and served with a potato or chestnut purée.

Coca: all-in-one dish. Thick pizza garnished in a host of different ways: typical topping consists of red bell peppers and black olives.

Cuinat: side dish. A purée of vegetables and pulses, broad beans, dried lupines, chard, the leaves of a wild plant known as *Lychnis*, and mint; usually eaten in springtime.

Empanadas: Folded-over pizzas containing fish, meat, or chard with pine nuts and raisins, sold in bakeries, pastry shops, and bars.

Ensaimadas: Round brioche made with a light pastry and filled with *cabellos de angel*, pumpkin jam.

Flaó: dessert. A tart garnished with a cream of fresh cheese, eggs, sugar, and mint.

Lentejas con sobrasada: starter. Lentils to which fried *sobrasada* is added.

Sopa seca mallorquina: starter. Similar to a pie, but cooked in a earthenware casserole dish. The ingredients are bread and vegetables.

Tombet de peix: main course. A kind of mixed timbale with fish and vegetables baked in the oven.

CANARY ISLANDS

Geographically distant from the rest of Spain, it is not surprising to find that the cuisine is exotic with North African influences. For this reason it is difficult to find a common link between the culinary traditions of the peninsula and these wonderful islands.

Escaldón canario: main course. Fricassee of vegetables mixed with *gofio* (toasted wheat flour prepared with water or milk, salt or sugar).

Puchero canario: all-in-one dish. A mixed broth of meat and vegetables: the main ingredients are beef, chick-peas, potatoes, salami, zucchini, cabbage, beans, and corn.

Sancocho canario: main course. A stew of dried salted cod, potatoes, and sweet potatoes that is served with *salsa de mojo*, a sauce of breadcrumbs seasoned with garlic, oil, vinegar and cumin.

Sopa del Teide: starter. Simple risotto with ripe tomatoes, onion, and garlic.

Tarta de plátanos: dessert. Little balls of banana, egg, cinnamon, and sugar, fried and covered with honey.

CASTILE-LEÓN

The gastronomic tradition of this region is firmly based on meat. Spring lamb and pig are the main ingredients of Castilian cuisine. However, fish are also an important element, obviously the freshwater kind and above all trout. Frogs and crabs are considered a great delicacy. Pork is the king of Castilian cuisine and there is no shortage of cold cuts and other pork cuts.

Arroz a la zamorana: starter. A fairly heavy dish, so much so that it is sometimes considered an all-in-one dish. It is a risotto cooked with parts of the pig such as the ear, snout, etc. to which are added onion, ham, and *navo* (a kind of celery).

Caldereta de Cordero: main course. A traditional dish cooked over a wood fire. The ingredients are pieces of spring lamb with brain, liver, and a host of spices.

Cangrejos de río (River crabs): starter. The crabs are cooked in a sauce of tomato, cognac, and abundant pepper and chili pepper.

Cochinillo asado: main course. Suckling pig roasted in lard.

Judiones de la granja: starter. Broad beans prepared with pig's trotter and ear plus small pieces of ham and salami.

Lechazo castellano: main course. Suckling lamb cooked in a earthenware saucepan with a little lard.

Sopa castellana: starter. A soup of bread with fried raw ham, beaten egg and abundant *pimentón*.

CASTILE-LA MANCHA, MADRID, ESTREMADURA

The cuisine of these regions shares some common characteristics. We have therefore decided to group them together. Here you will find those farmhouse recipes of olden times that are followed to the letter. Without a doubt, these are what Spanish cuisine truly stands for.

Besugo a la madrileña (Sea bream a la madrilena): main course. Baked in the oven and served with a tomato purée.

Cazuela extremeña: main course. Pork stewed with *chorizo*, bell peppers, tomato and garlic.

Caldereta extremeña: main course. Kid or lamb and calf's liver simmered with onion, garlic, red win and flour, to thicken the sauce.

Callos a la madrileña: main course. Ox tripe, *chorizo*, *morcilla*, and ham cooked in oil, lard and white wine with onions, carrots, garlic, herbs, and spices.

Cocido madrileño (or **castellano**): main course. A dish of mixed boiled meats (chicken, breast, pig's trotters, ears, *morcilla*) with boiled vegetables served separately, carrots, potatoes, cabbage, onion, celery, and leeks, chick-peas in their own liquid. The broth is served in a tureen with *fideos* (fine noodles chopped into shorter lengths).

Gratinado de berenjenas: (Eggplant au gratin): side dish. Sliced eggplant covered in grated cheese and cooked in the oven.

Las mijas: dessert. Crustless bread fried in butter with raisins.

Lentejas al estilo de Burgos: main course. A stew of lentils and *morcilla* from the city of Burgos that is made from pig's blood, chopped onion and rice.

Morteruolo: a very particular dish. The ingredients are pieces of hare, chicken, pig's liver, lard, and cinnamon; they are all cooked together then finely chopped and covered in more lard.

Perdiz estofada: main course. Casseroled partridge with potatoes.

Pisto manchego: main course. Mixed fry of red bell peppers, potatoes, zucchini, tomatoes, and bacon.

Rebado de Cáceres: starter. Dried salted cod with potatoes and chopped hard-boiled egg yolks.

CATALONIA

Catalonian cuisine differs from that of the other regions since it is particularly rich in products from both sea and mountain: from fish to meat including game; from vegetables to rich salads, not to mention the wide variety of sliced ham and cold cuts.

Conejo con peras (Rabbit and pears): main course. Small pieces of rabbit with a sauce of carrots, pears, leeks, and celery.

Escalvida: side dish. A selection of fried vegetables with bell peppers, eggplant, tomatoes, onions, potatoes, vinegar, and pepper.

Escudella i carn d'olla: all-in-one dish. This dish is made up of two parts. *Escudella* is a mixture of boiled meats (beef, pork, *butifarra*, etc.) with carrots, celery, chick-peas, potatoes, and cabbage; *pelota*, on the other hand, is a sort of meatball of lean minced meat with pepper, garlic, parsley, bread, flour, and salt, that is added to the *escudella* just before cooking is complete.

Suquet de peix: main course. A delicious selection of fish and shellfish served with a special almond sauce, fried bread, and liver of angler fish.

GALICIA

From a gastronomic point of view, this region is often considered the home of seafood. Whilst this is certainly the case, other treats are also in store. Besides the specialties of fish, you will often find meat, and, in particular, game.

The salmon is quite excellent, as is the sea trout and red meat. In homes and restaurants there is no shortage of wonderful dishes of game such as duck or loin of wild boar.

Besides all this, pastries are absolutely delicious, in particular *las filloas*, that are a typical carnival dessert.

Caldeirada (o caldareta) de pescado: starter. A fish soup that consists of mackerel and angler fish cooked in white wine with garlic, tomato, and saffron; it is served with toasted bread.

Caldo gallego (Galician broth): starter. Two varieties of this broth exist; one vegetable, whilst the other is a lot richer and contains pig's tail and ear, *lacón* and the famous Galician variety of *chorizos*.

In the vegetable variety we find savoy, broad beans, beans, and potatoes. This special dish is somewhat heavy and whilst considered a starter, it could also be an all-in-one dish.

Empanada gallega: all-in-one dish. Savory pie filled with tuna or meat, vegetables, bell peppers, olives.

Filloas: dessert. Like *frixuelos* (see page 42), they are very thin *crêpes* filled with cream or pig's blood. It was originally is a dish traditionally eaten at carnival time.

Lacón con grelos: all-in-one dish. A heavy, spicy dish due to the presence of *lacón* with turnips, salami, pig's ear, and potatoes that are all boiled together. A traditional dish that is usually eaten in wintertime.

Mejillones al vino blanco (Mussels in white wine sauce): hors-d'oeuvre. Boiled mussels with a sauce of garlic, parsley, and white wine.

Pulpo afeira: main course. Octopus cooked in a previously prepared mixture of oil, garlic, hot and mild paprika, and left to brown.

Rape a la gallega (Galician style angler fish): main course. Angler fish cooked with potatoes, onion, and bay leaf.

Reo con almejas (Sea trout and clams): main course. The fish is cooked with wine and clams and is filleted and cut into slices before serving.

Salmón a noso estilo (Salmon): main course. Oven-baked salmon with mushrooms, meat stock, orange juice, and Tabasco sauce. It is served with a slice of raw ham on top.

Vieiras con col: main course. The shellfish are grilled, whilst the savoy cabbage is cooked with butter and white wine. Everything is then put in the oven before serving.

BASQUE COUNTRY

Both national and international opinion have awarded Basque cuisine the number one spot on the Iberian peninsula.
A distinction can be made between the cuisine of the coastal areas, that is mainly fish-based (the most important ingredient being dried salted cod), and the inland cuisine that is heavily based on meat.
Besides these two important branches, there is also that

modern school known as *nouvelle cuisine,* a polished abstract of the region's gastronomic tradition, that has taken Basque chefs to the top of the culinary tree.

Angulas a la vasca (Basque-style eel fry): main course. The tiny eels are cooked one by one with garlic. Chili pepper is added afterwards. They are served together on a single plate.

Bacalao al pil pil (Dried salted cod) main course. This dish is served with a creamy sauce which is made by patiently stirring the ingredients in a saucepan. Essential for this delicious cream is the jelly obtained from the skin of the dried salted cod.

Bacalao a la vizcaina: main course. The dried salted cod is cooked in an earthenware pot with abundant onion and garlic. Hard-boiled egg yolks are also added.

Cordero en chilindrón: main course. Fricassee of lamb (or chicken) in a spicy sauce of onion, garlic, and thin strips of pepper.

Chipirones en su tinta: main course. *chipirón* is the name given to a small squid that is cooked in its own black ink sauce and served with rice.

Chipirones rellenos: main course. The same small squid filled with onion, bell peppers, tomato, breadcrumbs, and garlic, stewed in their own black ink sauce.

Gallina en pepitoria: main course. Fricassee of chicken in lard and oil with diced Sierra ham, white wine, and aromatic herbs. It is served with a sauce made from the juices accumulated during cooking mixed with egg yolk, garlic, and ground almonds.

Merluza a la vasca: main course. Slices of hake with prawns and clams in a thick white wine sauce, garlic, and parsley, garnished with boiled eggs, asparagus, and peas.

Perdices con chocolate: main course. Partridge in a sauce of cocoa, white wine, cloves, and other spices.

Purrusalda: main course. Dried salted cod with leeks and potatoes, and cooked in an earthenware casserole dish.

Txangurro relleno: (Stuffed *centollo*) starter. The meat of this sea crab is cooked with cognac, butter, tomato, salt, and pepper. The mixture is then put back into the shell and served.

LA RIOJA, ARAGÓN, NAVARRA

These three regions each have a different cuisine, but share many common characteristics, since the basic ingredients of all three are mutton and poultry along with vegetable produce. The trout, a freshwater fish typical of these parts, is now established at a national level. The spring lamb also has an important role, without forgetting the famous Navarra asparagus.

Caracoles a la riojana (Snails): main course. A dish peculiar to this region. The snails are cooked in a sauce of tomato, bell peppers, and ham.

Cochifrito: main course. Pieces of spring lamb fried with abundant onion and garlic. Added spices are pepper and *pimentón*. The lamb is served without a sauce.

Chuletas a la aragonesa: main course. Pork chops floured and browned in lard with garlic, white wine, chopped hard-boiled eggs, and tomato purée.

Hinojos con jamón: (Fennel and ham): main course. Fried and scrambled eggs with fennel and ham.

Judías con chorizo: main course. Butter beans cooked in lard with potatoes, pieces of salami, onions, and garlic.

Olla podrida: starter. A hearty soup of mixed meats, pork, chicken, partridge, *chorizo*, lard, and bacon, with vegetables.

Patatas a la riojana: main course. Potatoes and *chorizo* browned in garlic, onion, and hot chili pepper.

Pencas de acelga gratinada: side dish. Chard stems are a traditional vegetable of central Spain; they are often cooked in the oven *au gratin* with béchamel and cheese.

Pochas a la Navarra: main course. *Pochas* is the local name for French beans cooked with tail of spring lamb in an earthenware casserole dish with a host of spices.

Pollo al chilindrón: main course. Small pieces of chicken with tomatoes, bell peppers, zucchini, eggplant, carrots, peas, and ham.

Recao de Binéfar: first course. A dish of butter beans, potatoes, rice, and a host of spices.

Truchas a la Navarra (Navarra-style trout): main course. Trout fried in lard together with a slice of raw ham. Served with a sprinkling of lemon.

VALENCIA AND MURCIA

Rice is the common characteristic linking the culinary traditions of Valencia and Murcia. In these regions the best risotto is to be found, preparad in a thousand different ways. This is the home of *paella*, the national dish. Besides the rice, we find dishes of fish and shellfish, but no less important is the meat, particularly the spring lamb. Game is also an important ingredient in the cuisine of these Mediterranean regions.

Arroz amb fesols y naps: starter. Rice with butter beans and turnips.

Arroz con costra: all-in-one dish. A risotto with chick-peas, chicken, *butifarra*, and eggs.

Buñuelos de manzanas: dessert. Apple fritters with brandy.

Dorada a la sal: main course. Gilthead bream baked in the oven with a covering of salt.

Fideua: all-in-one dish. Risotto containing various types of fish with a sauce of almonds, bread, saffron and *pimentón*. Everything is then mixed with potatoes and onions.

Guisado de trigo: main course. A roast of chick-peas, potatoes, French beans, zucchini, tomatoes and a host of spices. This dish was traditionally eaten on Maundy Thursday (the Thursday before Easter).

Paella a la valenciana: all-in-one dish or main course. Huge dish of mussels, crabs or king prawns, cuttlefish, boiled chicken and its broth, diced ham, peas, French beans, tomatoes, garlic, saffron, herbs, and spices; the rice is added towards the end of cooking.

Pestiños: dessert. A kind of croissant that is fried and soaked with honey. Traditionally eaten at Easter.

Salpicón de Murcia: main course. Barbecued dried salted cod, which is then finely chopped, cooked with potatoes, and covered in a sauce of onion, parsley, garlic, oil, and vinegar.

The definitions listed in this chapter are those generally used in restaurants throughout Spain to indicate the most common methods of cooking and preparation that characterize the country's best-known dishes.

Al agridulce: This can readily be translated as "sweet-and-sour" and is used to indicate that the sauce contains both vinegar and sugar.

Ali-oli: Typical of the Catalonia region, but may now be found throughout the peninsula. It is a kind of thin mayonnaise with abundant chopped garlic.

A la campesina: generic term for a farmhouse-style dish containing full-flavored ingredients.

A la cazuela: indicates that the dish is cooked over a low heat in a earthenware casserole dish.

Al gratén: the Spanish equivalent of the commonly used French term *au gratin*. The term is used to indicate the method of preparation of various dishes. The food is covered in béchamel or breadcrumbs and cooked in the oven until forming a light golden crust.

A las hierbas: expression used when the dish is prepared with an abundance of mixed herbs and spices.

Al horno: term used to describe any dish that is cooked in the oven.

A la importancia: term used exclusively for potatoes and which merely means "French fries."

A la jardinera: this term means that vegetables are added to the main ingredient and is often used in the case of soups.

Al Jerez: used to describe a dish cooked in the famous wine from Andalusia.

A la marinera: used to describe a dish whose ingredients include fish or other seafood.

Al natural: For our translation we must once again use a borrowed French term: *au naturel*. This may be used to describe a food that is uncooked, or cooked in the most natural or simplest way without additional ingredients.

A la parrilla: this merely means that the food is grilled and it is used for meat, fish and seafood.

Al plato: besides indicating the presence of eggs, this term is used to show that the food will be served in the same casserole dish in which it was cooked.

Al vapor: this means that the food is steamed and is used for vegetables, and sometimes shellfish, such as mussels and clams.

A la vinagreta: a sauce of onion, oil, vinegar, parsley, and hard-boiled egg.

Bocadillo: any type of bread roll.

De la casa: specialties of the house exclusive to a particular restaurant. It is worth asking the waiter to explain what they are. When referring to wine, it indicates that it will be served in a carafe or has been produced by the restaurant itself.

En almíbar: term used to describe any kind of tinned fruit in syrup. Also used for *torrijas* (see page 22), although in this case the exact term is *in almíbar*.

En escabeche: pickled in vinegar.

En rodajas: indicates any type of food served in thin slices.

En salsa tártara: Used for fish dishes and merely means "served with a tartar sauce."

En salsa verde: sauce used for meat and fish-based recipes. A simple recipe of oil, salt, and parsley.

En su tinta: term used for cuttlefish and squid that are cooked in their own black ink sauce.

Fiambre: a selection of any type of sliced ham or cold cuts.

Pinchos: small rolls to be found in any bar or coffee shop.

Plato combinado: term used to describe a simple mixed platter that can contain eggs, potatoes, salad, slices of meat, etc. This type of dish is commonly served in bars and coffee shops.

Relleno/a: any type of dish with a stuffing or filling.

Revuelto: indicates the presence of scrambled eggs mixed with some other ingredient such as asparagus, prawns, etc.

Vegetariano: this definition can be applied to a whole host of different recipes, but in every case it refers to vegetable-based dishes that do not contain meat, fish or cold cuts.

ALMEJAS A LA MARINERA

Ingredients:

clams	2 lb 3 oz	(1 kg)
garlic	2 cloves	
onion	1	
flour	1 tablespoon	
white wine	1 glass	
white pepper, parsley, salt, olive oil		

Method:

Leave the clams to soak in salted water for a couple of hours, thus ensuring that all sand is removed.
Heat a little olive oil in a earthenware casserole dish; add chopped garlic and onion.
Allow to brown over a moderate flame.
Add flour, white wine, and a little water. Increase the heat and allow to boil.
Add the clams and cover with a lid so that the steam opens the clams.
Stir, taste, and when cooked add salt, pepper, and parsley.
Serve at once.

Note: All recipes serve four.

Caldo Gallego

Ingredients:

water	6 pints	(3 liters)
ham bone	1	
veal bone	1	
haricot beans	4 oz	(100 g)
sliced potatoes	2 lb 3 oz	(1 kg)
fat	1 oz	(25 g)
a little cabbage or savoy		
(other vegetables as desired)		

Method:

Place the bones and haricot beans in a large saucepan with salted water. When the beans are half-cooked, remove the bones, add the potatoes, and leave to cook. In another saucepan, place the savoy and other chosen vegetables and bring to the boil. Then place the vegetables in the first saucepan and mix with the potatoes and beans. Finally, add the fat and allow to cook well.

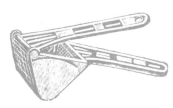

CALLOS

Ingredients:

tripe	2 lb 3 oz	(1 kg)
onion	1/2	
flour	1 tablespoon	
mild pimentón	1 tablespoon	
hot pimentón	1 tablespoon	
garlic, tomato, a little lard, salt		

Method:

Cut the tripe into small pieces and leave to boil in a saucepan containing plenty of water. When the tripe is almost cooked, prepare a frying pan with a little lard, tomato, chopped garlic and onion, mild *pimentón*, hot *pimentón*, and the flour. Allow to fry until brown. Add the tripe and a little of its cooking water and leave until cooking is complete.

COCIDO MADRILEÑO

Ingredients:

chick peas	*1 lb*	*(1/2 kg)*
cabbage or savoy		
pork bone	*1*	
red salami sausage	*1*	
mixed meat	*11 oz*	*(300 g)*
thin pasta, a little lard, salt		

Method:

Place all the ingredients, except the pasta, in a pressure cooker and allow to boil for 30 minutes. Using the broth obtained, prepare a soup adding a thin type of pasta (either the long or short variety is OK). Serve the other ingredients on a separate platter with some olive oil.

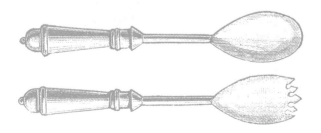

FABADA ASTURIANA

Ingredients:

pig's trotter	1	
salted pork	1 lb	(1/2 kg)
pig's ear	1	
butter beans	2 lb 3 oz	(1 kg)
red salami sausages	3	
morcillas	3	
lard, salt, garlic, bay leaf		

Method:

Leave the trotter, meat, and ear to soak for 12 hours (change the water at least once). Transfer everything to a saucepan with the salami sausages, *morcillas*, and lard. Cover with a layer of butter beans and add chopped garlic, parsley, and quartered onion. Cover with cold water and bring to a boil, then reduce heat and cook slowly.

The beans should remain covered, so add more cold water if necessary. Cook until the beans are tender, and add a knob of butter before serving.

MERLUZA A LA CAZUELA

Ingredients:

sliced hake	1 lb 6 oz	(600 g)
clams	11 oz	(300 g)
prawns	4 oz	(100 g)
white wine	1 glass	
flour	1 tablespoon	
onion, garlic, pimentón, bay leaf, salt, olive oil		

Method:

Heat the oil in an earthenware casserole dish, add the garlic and onion, and allow to fry until brown; then add the clams and prawns and wait for the clams to open. Add the hake, *pimentón*, flour, bay leaf, and wine. Leave to cook over a moderate flame, and when cooking is complete, garnish with asparagus, bell peppers, and a sprig of parsley.

Paella Valenciana

Ingredients:

rice	7 oz	(200 g)
(1 coffee cup per person)		
clams	9 oz	(250 g)
prawns	5 oz	(150 g)
cuttlefish cut into		
small pieces	5 oz	(150 g)
mussels	5 oz	(150 g)
bell peppers	2 oz	(50 g)
peas	2 oz	(50 g)
finely chopped tomatoes	2	
sachets saffron	3	
finely chopped onion	1	
garlic cloves	2	
salt		
stock cube	1	

Method:

Boil the mussels separately. When cooked, remove one half of each shell for decoration. In a large shallow pan (so much the better if you have the proper *paellera* that is specially designed for this dish) heat the oil and fry onion, garlic, parsley, and the tomatoes.

Once they are golden brown, add the prawns (leaving aside 4 of them for final decoration), the chopped cuttlefish, and the clams, and cook until the latter have opened.

Then add the bell peppers (that have been boiled beforehand), peas, and water: the secret of cooking the *paella* lies right here: three parts of water to one part of rice.

Add salt, the sachets of saffron, and the stock cube. When the water begins to boil, introduce the rice.

Important tip: the rice must on no account be stirred with a spoon. Instead, clasp the pan firmly by the handles, mixing the rice in a circular movement. Cooking time is about 30 minutes, but the *paella* will only be ready when all the water has evaporated.

Ten minutes before the end of cooking, arrange the remaining prawns and mussels as decoration. Slices of hard-boiled egg can also be added if desired. Serve at once.

Mixed paella also contains pieces of meat (chicken, beef, rabbit, etc. as desired) that are cooked separately and added just before the rice itself is fully cooked.

Tortilla Española

Ingredients:

thinly sliced potatoes	3 lb 4 oz	(1 1/2 kg)
chopped onion	1	
eggs	4	
salt, olive oil		

Method:

Fry the potatoes and onion in a frying pan with a generous amount of olive oil. Beat the eggs in a bowl with a little salt. When the potatoes are cooked, transfer them to the bowl. Remove all the oil from the frying pan and introduce the mixture which should be cooked until golden brown on both sides. Serve at once.
If you want to try *tortilla paisana*, just fry a few zucchini and bell peppers along with the potatoes.

A como en **Antonio**
ah kohmoh ayn ahntohnyoh

B Barcelona
bay bahrtheh<u>loh</u>nah

C Carmen
thay <u>kahr</u>mayn

CH Chocolate
chay chohkoh<u>lah</u>tay

D Dolores
day doh<u>loh</u>rays

E Enrique
ay ayn<u>ree</u>kay

F Francia
eh<u>fay frah</u>nthyah

G Gerona
khay kheh<u>roh</u>nah

H Historia
<u>a</u>chay ees<u>toh</u>ryah

I Inés
ee ee<u>nays</u>

J José
<u>kho</u>ta khoh<u>say</u>

K Kilo
ka <u>kee</u>loh

L Lorenzo
eh<u>lay</u> loh<u>ray</u>nthoh

LL Llobregat
ay<u>lyay</u> lyohbray<u>gaht</u>

M Madrid
eh<u>may</u> mah<u>dreedh</u>

N Navarra
eh<u>nay</u> nah<u>vah</u>rrah

Ñ Ñoño
ay<u>nyay</u> <u>nioh</u>nioh

O Oviedo
oh oh<u>vyay</u>dhoh

P París
pay pah<u>rees</u>

Q Querido
koo kay<u>reed</u>hoh

R Ramón
eh<u>ray</u> rah<u>mon</u>

S Sábado
eh<u>say</u> <u>sah</u>bhahdhoh

T Tortilla
tay tor<u>tee</u>lyah

U Ulises
oo oo<u>lee</u>says

V Valencia
<u>oo</u>bay bah<u>layn</u>thyah

W Washington
<u>oo</u>blay <u>doh</u>blay <u>wah</u>zeenton

X Xiquena
<u>ay</u>kees ksee<u>kay</u>nah

Y Yegua
ee gree<u>ay</u>ga <u>yeh</u>khwah

Z Zumo
<u>thay</u>tah <u>thoo</u>moh

Things to remember

If you want to purchase cheese or cold cuts, your best bet are the charcuterias. *For other local products (wines, olive oil, etc.) the big supermarkets offer good quality and value for money.*

Is this cheese fresh?	**¿Es fresco este queso?** *Ays frayhskoh aystay kaysoh?*
How much does it cost per kilo?	**¿Cuánto cuesta al quilo?** *Kwahntoh kwaystah ahl keeloh?*
How long will it keep?	**¿Cuánto tiempo dura conservado?** *Kwahntoh tyaympoh doorah kohnsayrbahdoh?*
I'll take this/that	**Me llevo esto/eso** *May lyayvoh aystoh/aysoh*
I'd like two bottles (of it)	**Querría/Quisiera dos botellas** *Kayrryah /Keesyayrah dos bohtaylyahs*
Give me half a kilo (of it)	**Déme medio quilo** *daymay maydhyoh keeloh*
Can you wrap it up for the journey?	**¿Me lo puede envolver para el viaje?** *May loh pwaydhay aynbohlvayr pahrah ayl beeahkhay?*

Things to remember

Cakeshops produce and sell a wide range of quality sweets and pastries which you will certainly want to try.

What are these/those?	**¿Qué son éstos / ésos?** *Kay son <u>ays</u>tohs / <u>ay</u>sohs?*
What's in this cake?	**¿Qué tiene esta tarta?** *Kay <u>tyay</u>nay <u>ays</u>tah <u>tah</u>rtah?*
I'd like a small/medium tray of pastries	**Quisiera una bandeja pequeña / media de pasteles** *Kee<u>sy</u>ayrah <u>oo</u>nah ban<u>day</u>khah pay<u>kay</u>niah/ <u>may</u>dhyah day pah<u>stay</u>lays*
I'd like an assortment of pastries	**Quisiera pastas variadas** *Kee<u>sy</u>ayrah <u>pahs</u>tahs vah<u>rya</u>hdhahs*
I'll have a 200-peseta cone, vanilla and chocolate with/without whipped cream	**Quisiera un cono de 200 pesetas con vainilla y chocolate con / sin nata** *Kee<u>sy</u>ayrah oon <u>koh</u>noh day dos<u>thyayn</u>tahs pay<u>say</u>tahs kon bigh<u>nee</u>lyah ee chohkoh<u>lah</u>tay kon / seen <u>nah</u>tah*
I'd like a 200-peseta ice-cream cup	**Quisiera una tarrina de helado de 200 pesetas** *Kee<u>sy</u>ayrah <u>oo</u>nah tah<u>rree</u>nah day ay<u>lah</u>dhoh day dos<u>thyayn</u>tahs pay<u>say</u>tahs*

I have a small child/two children
Tengo un niño pequeño/dos niños
Tayngoh oon neenioh paykaynioh / dos neeniohs

Do you have a special rate for children?
¿Hacen precios reducidos para niños?
Ahthen praythyohs raydootheedohs pahrah neeniohs?

Do you have a cot/high chair for the baby?
¿Tienen una cuna/una silla para el niño?
Tyaynayn oonah koonah/oonah seelyah pahrah ayl neenioh?

Is there a children's menu?
¿Tienen un menú para niños?
¿Tyaynayn oon maynoo pahrah neeniohs?

Can you warm the baby's bottle?
¿Puede calentarme el biberón para el niño?
Pwaydhay kahlayntahrmay ayl beebhayron pahrah ayl neenioh?

Where can I feed/change the baby?
¿Dónde puedo dar la leche / cambiar al niño?
¿Dohnday pwaydhoh dahr lah laychay/kahmbyahr ahl neenioh?

Is there a park where the children can play?
¿Hay un parque donde los niños puedan ir a jugar?
Igh oon pahrkay dohnday los neeniohs pwaydhahn eer ah khoogahr?

This doesn't work

Esto no funciona
Aystoh noh foonthyonah

It's faulty

Tiene algún defecto
Tyaynay ahlgoon dayfehktoh

We are still waiting to be served

Estamos todavía esperando que nos sirvan
Aystahmohs tohdhahveeah ayspayrahndoh kay nohs seervahn

The coffee is cold

El café está frío
Ayl kahfay aystah freeoh

The tablecloth is dirty

El mantel no está limpio
Ayl mahntayl noh aystah leempyoh

The room is noisy

En esta habitación se oyen todos los ruidos
Ayn aystah ahbheetahthyon say ohyayn tohdhohs los rooeedhos

It's too smoky here

Aquí hay demasiado humo
Ahkee igh daymahsyahdhoh oomoh

Do you speak English?	**¿Habla inglés?** *Ahblah eenglays?*
I don't speak Spanish	**No hablo español** *Noh ahbloh ayspahniol*
What's your name?	**¿Cómo se llama / te llamas?** *Kohmoh say lyahmah / tay lyahmahs?*
My name is...	**Me llamo...** *May lyahmoh...*
Do you mind if I sit here?	**¿Le importa si me siento aquí?** *Lay eempohrtah see may syayntoh ahkee?*
Is this place free?	**¿Está libre este sitio?** *Aystah leebray aystay seetyoh?*
Where are you from?	**¿De dónde es?** *Day dohnday ays?*
I'm from...	**Soy de...** *Soy day...*
I'm English/American/ Spanish	**Soy inglés, americanos, español** *Soy eenglays, ahmayreekahnohs, ayspahniol*
Can I offer you a coffee/ something to drink?	**¿Puedo invitarle a un café /algo de beber?** *Pwaydoh eenbeetahrlay ah oon kahfay/ahlgoh day baybhayr?*

Things to remember

The peseta is the local currency with bank notes available in the following denominations: 10,000 - 5,000 - 2,000 - 1,000. The range of coins is as follows: 500 - 200 - 100 - 50 - 25 - 5. You may occasionally find coins of a lesser value but they are virtually worthless.

I don't have enough money

No tengo bastante dinero
Noh tayngoh bahstahntay deenayroh

Do you have any change?

¿Tienen para cambiar?
Tyaynayn pahrah kahmbyahr?

Can you change a ten-thousand-peseta note?

¿Me puede cambiar un billete de 10.000 pesetas?
May pwaydhay kahmbyahr oon beelyaytay day dyayth meel paysaytahs?

I'd like to change these dollars/francs/sterling into pesetas

Quisiera cambiar estos dólares/ francos/estas esterlinas en pesetas
Keesyayrah kahmbyahr aystohs dohlahrays/frahnkos/aystahs aystayrleenahs ayn paysaytahs

What is the rate for sterling/dollars/francs...?

¿A cuánto está el cambio de las esterlinas/los dólares/los francos...?
Ah kwahntoh aystah ayl kahmbyoh day lahs aystayrleenahs/los dohlahrays/los frahnkos?

| First of March | **El 1 de marzo** |
| | *Ayl oonoh day mahrthoh* |

| Second of June | **Dos de junio** |
| | *Dos day khoonyoh* |

| We will be arriving on the 29th of August | **Llegaremos el 29 de agosto** |
| | *Lyaygahraymohs ayl 29 day ahgohstoh* |

| Nineteen ninety-seven | **Mil novecientos noventa y siete** |
| | *Meel nohvaythyayntohs nohbayntah ee seeaytay* |

Sunday	**domingo**	*dohmeengoh*
Monday	**lunes**	*loonays*
Tuesday	**martes**	*mahrtays*
Wednesday	**miércoles**	*myayrkohlays*
Thursday	**jueves**	*khwayvays*
Friday	**viernes**	*byayrnays*
Saturday	**sábado**	*sahbhadhoh*

January	**enero**	*aynayroh*
February	**febrero**	*fehbrehroh*
March	**marzo**	*mahrthoh*
April	**abril**	*ahbreel*
May	**mayo**	*mahyoh*
June	**junio**	*khoonyoh*
July	**julio**	*khoolyoh*
August	**agosto**	*ahgohstoh*
September	**septiembre**	*sehptyaymbray*
October	**octubre**	*oktoobray*
November	**noviembre**	*nohvyaymbray*
December	**diciembre**	*deethyaymbray*

Excuse me, where is the station?

¿Perdone, dónde está la estación?
Pehrdohnay dohnday aystah lah aystahthyon?

How do I get to the airport?

¿Cómo tengo que hacer para ir al aeropuerto?
Kohmoh tayngoh kay ahthehr pahrah eer ahl ahayrohpwayrtoh?

Is this the road that leads to Plaza Mayor?

¿Es ésta la calle que va a la Plaza Mayor?
Ays aystah lah kahlyay kay vah ah lah plahthah mahyohr?

I'm looking for the tourist information office

Estoy buscando la oficina de Información Turística
Aystoy booskahndoh lah ohfeetheenah day eenformahthyon tooreesteekah

How long does it take to get there?

¿Cuánto se tarda en llegar?
Kwahntoh say tahrdah ayn lyaygahr?

Excuse me, can you tell me where the... restaurant is?

¿Perdone, me puede decir dónde está el restaurante...?
Pehrdohnay, may pwaydhay daytheer dohnday aystah ayl raystowrahntay...?

Things to remember

Besides coffee and other drinks, cafés also offer a selection
of filled rolls, tapas, mixed platters, and pastries.

A black coffee/ cappuccino	**Un café solo / un café con leche** *Oon kahfay sohloh / oon kahfay kon laychay*
A draught beer	**Una cerveza de barril / una caña** *Oonah thehrbaythah day bahrreel/ oonah kahniah*
A medium lager/stout	**Una cerveza clara / oscura / media** *Oonah thehrbaythah klahrah ohskoorah/maydhyah*
Two cups of tea with milk	**Dos tazas de té con leche** *Dos tahthahs day tay kon laychay*
A glass of mineral water	**Un vaso de agua mineral** *Oon bahsoh day ahgwah meenayrahl*
With ice, please	**Con hielo, por favor** *Kon yayloh, por fahvor*
Another coffee, please	**Por favor, otro café** *Por fahvor, ohtroh kahfay*
Bring me the bill, please	**Tráigame la cuenta, por favor** *Trighgahmay lah kwayntah, por fahvor*

Things to remember

Besides proper restaurants, there is also a range of other eating places including the bodegas, tascas, tabernas, and mesones (small family-run restaurants).

Is there a good restaurant around here?

¿Hay un buen restaurante por aquí?
Igh oon bwayn raystowrahntay por ahkee?

Is there a cheap restaurant nearby?

¿Hay un restaurante barato por aquí cerca?
Igh oon raystowrahntay bahrahtoh por ahkee thehrkah?

Do you know of a restaurant with local cuisine?

¿Puede indicarme dónde hay un restaurante que sirva comidas típicas?
Pwaydhay eendeekahrmay dohnday igh oon raystowrahntay kay seervah kohmeedhahs teepeekahs?

How does one get there?

¿Cómo se llega?
Kohmoh say lyaygah?

Excuse me, can you tell me where is the ... restaurant?

¿Perdone, me puede indicar dónde está el restaurante...?
Pehrdohnay, may pwaydhay eendeekahr dohnday aystah ayl raystowrahntay...?

Which is the best restaurant in town?

¿Cuál es el mejor restaurante de la ciudad?
Kwahl ays ayl meh<u>khor</u> raystow<u>rahn</u>tay day lah thyoo<u>dhahdh</u>?

We'd like to eat in a cheap restaurant

Queríamos comer en un restaurante que costase poco
Kay<u>ree</u>ahmohs koh<u>mehr</u> ayn oon raystow<u>rahn</u>tay kay cos<u>tá</u>se <u>poh</u>koh

Is it possible to book a table for four please?

¿Se puede reservar una mesa para cuatro?
Say <u>pway</u>dhay rehsayr<u>bahr</u> oonah <u>may</u>sah pahrah <u>kwah</u>troh?

I'd like to book a table for two people, for this evening/tomorrow evening at 8:00, in the name of...

Quisiera reservar una mesa para dos personas, para esta noche/mañana por la noche a las ocho a nombre de...
Kee<u>syay</u>rah rehsayr<u>bahr</u> oonah <u>may</u>sah pahrah dos payr<u>soh</u>nahs, pahrah <u>ays</u>tah <u>noh</u>chay/ mah<u>nia</u>hnah por lah <u>noh</u>chay ah lahs <u>oh</u>choh ah <u>nohm</u>bray day...

What day are you closed?

¿Cuándo es el día de descanso semanal?
<u>Kwahn</u>doh ays ayl <u>dee</u>ah day des<u>cah</u>nso semah<u>nahl</u>?

What time does the restaurant open/close?

¿A qué hora abre / cierra el restaurante?
Ah kay ohrah ahbray / thyehrrah ayl raystowrahntay?

I'd like to cancel a booking I made for this evening, for two people, in the name of...

Quisiera anular una reserva que había hecho para esta noche, para dos personas, a nombre de...
Keesyayrah ahnoolahr oonah rehsehrbah kay ahbeeah aychoh pahrah aystah nohchay, pahrah dos payrsohnahs, ah nohmbray day..

Is it necessary to reserve?

¿Es necesario reservar mesa?
Ays naythaysahryoh rehsayrbahr maysah?

Good evening, a table for two

Buenas noches, una mesa para dos
Bwaynohs nohchays, oonah maysah pahrah dos

We'd like a table in a quiet corner

Queríamos una mesa en un sitio tranquilo
Kayreeahmohs oonah maysah ayn oon seetyoh trahnkeeloh

We've booked a table for two in the name of...

Hemos reservado una mesa para dos, a nombre de...
Ehmohs rehsehrbahdhoh oonah maysah pahrah dos, ah nohmbray day...

Can one eat outside?	**¿Se puede comer fuera / al aire libre?** *Say pwaydhay kohmehr fwayrah / ahl ighray leebray?*
We'd like a table away from/next to the window	**Queríamos una mesa lejos de / cerca de la ventana** *Kayreeahmohs oonah maysah lehkos day/thehrkah day lah behntahnah*
Is there an entrance for the disabled?	**¿Hay una entrada para minusválidos?** *Igh oonah ayntradhah pahrah meenoosbahleedohs?*
Do you speak English, French...?	**¿Habla inglés, francés...?** *Ahblah eenglays, frahnthays...?*
Is there a fixed-price menu?	**¿Tienen un menú con precio único?** *Tyaynayn oon maynoo kon praythyoh ooneekoh?*
Can we see the menu?	**¿Podemos ver la carta?** *Pohdehmohs behr lah kahrtah?*
Is there is vegetarian menu?	**¿Tienen un menú vegetariano?** *Tyaynayn oon maynoo baykhaytahryahnoh?*
What is the specialty of the house?	**¿Cuál es la especialidad de la casa?** *Kwahl ays lah ayspehthyahleedhahdh day la kahsah?*

What is the dish of the day?

¿Cuál es el plato del día?
Kwahl ays ayl plahtoh dayl deeah?

What do you recommend?

¿Qué nos recomienda?
Kay nohs rehkohmyayndah?

What's in this dish?

¿Qué lleva / tiene el plato?
Kay lyayvah / tyaynay ayl plahtoh?

Is it spicy?

¿Pica?
Peekah?

I'm allergic to peppers

Soy alérgico al pimiento
Soy ahlehrkheekoh ahl peemyayntoh

Is there garlic/pepper in this dish?

¿Este plato lleva ajo / pimienta?
Aystay plahtoh lyayvah ahkhoh / peemyayntah?

Do you have...?

¿Tienen...?
Tyaynayn...?

I'd like/We'd like...

Quisiera / Quisiéramos...
Keesyayrah / Keesyayrahmohs...

Can you bring me/us...?

Tráigame / nos...
Trighgahmay/ nohs...

I would like a portion/half a portion of...

Quisiera una ración / media ración de...
Keesyayrah oonah rahthyon/ maydhyah rahthyon day...

I'd like to taste...

Quisiera probar...
Keesyayrah provahr...

Can you bring us some more bread please?

¿Puede traernos más pan, por favor?
Pwaydhay trahehrnohs mahs pahn, por fahvor

What are the typical local dishes?

¿Cuáles son los platos típicos de la zona?
Kwahlays son los plahtohs teepeekohs day lah thohnah?

What is the typical local cheese?

¿Cuál es el queso típico de la zona?
Kwahl ays ayl kaysoh teepeekoh day lah thohnah?

What dessert/fruit do you have?

¿Qué postres / fruta tienen?
Kay pohstrays/ frootah tyaynayn?

We'd like a portion of... and two plates

Queríamos una ración de... con dos platos
Kayreeahmohs oonah rahthyon day... kon dos plahtohs

Could I have the salt/ pepper?

¿Me puede traer la sal / la pimienta?
May pwaydhay trahehr lah sahl / lah peemyayntah?

Four coffees, please

Cuatro cafés, por favor
Kwahtroh kahfays, por fahvor

What starters are there?

¿Qué entremeses tienen?
Kay ayntraymaysays tyaynayn?

I'd like this dish, but without onions

Está bien este plato, pero sin cebollas
Aystah byayn aystay plahtoh, payroh seen thaybohlyahs

Can you change the... for...?

¿Puede cambiar el... por...?
Pwaydhay kahmbyahr ayl... por...?

Can we see the wine list?

¿Podemos ver la carta de vinos?
Pohdehmohs behr lah kahrtah day beenohs?

We'd like an aperitif

Querémos un aperitivo/vermouth
Kayraymohs oon ahpayreeteevoh / behrmoot

What wine would you recommend with this dish?

¿Qué vino nos recomienda para este plato?
Kay beenoh nohs rehkohmyayndah pahrah aystay plahtoh?

Can you recommend a good white/red/rosé wine?

Recomiéndenos un buen vino blanco / tinto / rosado
rehkohmyayndaynohs oon bwayn beenoh blahnkoh/ teentoh/ rosahdhoh

We'd like the house wine, please

Tráiganos el vino de la casa, por favor
Trighgahnohs ayl beenoh day lah kahsah, por fahvor

A/Half a bottle of...

Una / Media botella de...
Oonah / maydhyah bohtaylyah day...

A bottle of natural/ sparkling mineral water, please

Por favor, una botella de agua mineral natural / con gas
Por fahvor, oonah bohtaylyah day ahgwah meenayrahl nahtoorahl / kon gas

We'd like some unchilled/chilled water

Queríamos agua del tiempo / del frigorífico
Kayreeahmohs ahgwah dayl tyaympoh/dayl treegohreefeekoh

Another bottle of water/ wine please

Por favor, tráiganos otra botella de agua /de vino
Por fahvor, trighgahnohs ohtrah bohtaylyah day ahgwah/ day beenoh

Which are the typical local wines/liqueurs?

¿Cuáles son los vinos / los licores típicos de la zona?
kwahlays son los beenohs / los leekohrays teepeekohs day lah thohnah?

What liqueurs do you have?

¿Qué licores tienen?
Kay leekohrays tyaynayn?

Could we have the bill, please?

La cuenta, por favor
Lah kwayntah, por fahvor

Excuse me, where is the restroom?	**¿Perdone, dónde está el baño?** *Pehr<u>doh</u>nay, <u>dohn</u>day ay<u>stah</u> ayl <u>bah</u>nioh?*
Can you bring me an ashtray / another glass / plate?	**¿Puede traerme un cenicero / otro vaso / plato?** *Pway<u>dhay</u> trahehr<u>may</u> oon thaynee<u>thay</u>roh /<u>oh</u>troh <u>bah</u>soh / <u>plah</u>toh?*
Can you change my fork/knife/spoon please?	**¿Me cambia el tenedor/el cuchillo/la cuchara, por favor?** *May <u>kahm</u>byah ayl taynay<u>dhohr</u>/ayl koo<u>chee</u>lyoh/lah koo<u>chah</u>rah, por fah<u>vor</u>*
Can you turn the air conditioning up/down?	**¿Se puede bajar / subir el aire acondicionado?** *Say <u>pway</u>dhay bah<u>khahr</u> / soo<u>bheer</u> ayl <u>igh</u>ray ahkohndeetheeohn<u>ah</u>doh?*
Is it possible to open/ close the window?	**¿Se puede abrir / cerrar la ventana?** *Say <u>pway</u>dhay ah<u>breer</u>/ thehr<u>rahr</u> lah behn<u>tah</u>nah?*
I've stained my clothes, have you got any talcum powder?	**Me he manchado, ¿tienen polvos de talco?** *May ay mahn<u>chah</u>dhoh, <u>tyay</u>nayn <u>pohl</u>bohs day <u>tahl</u>koh?*
Could you call us a taxi please?	**¿Puede llamarnos a un taxi, por favor?** *Pway<u>dhay</u> lyah<u>mahr</u>nohs ah oon <u>tahk</u>see, por fah<u>vor</u>?*

Is there a doctor here?

¿Hay un médico aquí?
Igh oon mehdheekoh ahkee?

Call a doctor/an
ambulance

**Llamad / llamen a un médico /
una ambulancia**
*Lyahmahdh/Lyahmayn ah oon
mehdheekoh/oonah
ahmboolahnthyah*

Go and get help,
quickly!

Id a pedir ayuda, ¡enseguida!
*eed ah pehdheer ahyoodhah,
aynsaygweedah!*

My wife is about to give
birth!

¡Mi mujer está pariendo!
*Mee mookhehr aystah
pahryayndoh!*

Where's the nearest
police station/hospital?

**¿Dónde está la policía / el
hospital más cercano?**
*Dohnday aystah lah pohleethyah/
ayl ohspeetahl mahs thehrkahnoh?*

I've lost my credit card/
wallet

**He perdido mi tarjeta de crédito /
la cartera**
*Ay pehrdeedhoh mee tahrkhaytah
day kraydheetoh/ lah kahrtayrah*

I've been robbed

Me han robado
May ahn rohbhahdhoh

My wallet has been
stolen

Me han robado la cartera
*May ahn rohbhahdhoh lah
kahrtayrah*

I've lost my child /
handbag

He perdido a mi hijo / el bolso
*Ay pehrdeedhoh ah mee eekhoh /
ayl bolsoh*

Are there any nightclubs/pubs?	**¿Hay locales nocturnos/pubs?**
	Igh lohkahlays nohktoornohs/pubs?

Is there a show/place suitable for children?	**¿Hay algún espectáculo/ sitio adecuado para niños?**
	Igh ahlgoon ayspehktahkooloh/ seeteeoh ahdhaykwahdoh pahrah neeniohs?

What is there to do in the evenings?	**¿Qué se puede hacer por la noche?**
	Kay say pwaydhay ahthehr por lah nohchay?

Where is there a cinema/theater?	**¿Dónde hay un cine/un teatro?**
	Dohnday igh oon theenay/ oon tayahtroh?

Can you book the tickets for us?	**¿Puede reservarnos las entradas?**
	Pwaydhay rehsayrbahrnohs lahs ayntradhahs?

Is there a swimming pool?	**¿Hay una piscina?**
	Igh oonah peestheenah?

Are there any good excursions to take?	**¿Hay buenas excursiones que hacer?**
	Igh bwaynahs exkoorsyohnays kay ahthehr?

Where can we play tennis/golf?	**¿Dónde podemos jugar a tenis/ a golf?**
	Dohnday pohdehmohs khoogahr ah taynees / ah golf?

Is there horseriding/fishing?	**¿Se puede ir a caballo / a pescar?**
	Say pwaydhay eer ah kahbhahlyoh / ah payskahr?

DEFINITE AND INDEFINITE ARTICLES

	Singular	*Plural*
the (M)	el	los
the (F)	la	las
a, some, any (M)	un	unos
a, some, any (F)	una	unas

NOUNS

As a rule, masculine singular nouns usually take the suffix **-o** (e.g. *chico*), whilst the feminine forms ends in **-a** (e.g. *chica*). However, certain masculine singular nouns end in **-e** (e.g. *padre*) or **-a** (e.g. *problema*).
There are also numerous nouns that finish in a consonant and may be either masculine (e.g. *camión, tenedor*) or feminine (e.g. *mujer, canción*).
The plural is formed as follows: nouns that end in a vowel take an **s** (e.g. *chico* becomes *chicos*), and those ending in a consonant take **es** (e.g. *camión* becomes *camiónes*).

ADJECTIVES

The adjective must agree with the noun (e.g. *chico simpático - chicos simpáticos - chica simpática - chicas simpáticas*).
There are also several adjectives ending in **-e** that do not change with gender (e.g. *chico alegre, chica alegre*).
The plural forms follow the above-mentioned rule.

POSSESSIVE ADJECTIVES

	Singular	Plural
my	mi	mis
your	tu	tus
his/her/its	su	sus
our	nuestro/nuestra	nuestros/nuestras
your	vuestro/vuestra	vuestros/vuestras
their	su	sus

Examples: mi casa, su tinta, vuestros pollos

POSSESSIVE PRONOUNS

	Singular		Plural	
	M	F	M	F
mine	el mio	la mia	los mios	las mias
yours	el tuyo	la tuya	los tuyos	las tuyas
his/hers/its	el suyo	la suya	los suyos	las suyas
ours	el nuestro	la nuestra	los nuestros	las nuestras
yours	el vuestro	la vuestra	los vuestros	las vuestras
theirs	el suyo	la suya	los suyos	las suyas

PRONOUNS

Subject	Direct Object	Indirect Object	Reflexive
yo	me	me / A mí	me
tú	te	te / A ti	te
él	lo	le / A él	se
ella	la	le / A ella	se
usted	le	le / A Usted	se

nosotros/as	nos	nos / A nosotros/as	os
vosotros/as	os	os / A vosotros/as	os
ellos	los	les / A ellos	se
ellas	las	les / A ella	se
ustedes	les	les / A ustedes	se

VERBS

Spanish verbs can be divided into three conjugations as can be seen from the three verbs indicated below as examples.

Simple present

Amar (to love)	Comer (to eat)	Escribir (to write)
am-o	com-o	escribo
am-as	com-es	escrib-es
am-a	com-e	escrib-e
am-amos	com-emos	escrib-imos
am-áis	com-éis	escrib-ís
am-an	com-en	escrib-en

Auxiliary verbs

Ser (to be)	Haber (to have)
soy	he
eres	has
es	ha
somos	hemos
sóis	habéis
son	han

Other useful verbs

Poder (to be able)	Ir (to go)	Ver (to see)
pued-o	voy	veo
pued-es	vas	ves
pued-e	va	ve
pod-emos	vamos	vemos
pod-éis	vais	veis
pued-en	van	ven

Perfect tense

Unlike other languages such as French and Italian, Spanish has only one auxiliary verb HABER (to have). The past participle is invariable.

he	amado	comido	escrito
has	amado	comido	escrito
ha	amado	comido	escrito
hemos	amado	comido	escrito
habéis	amado	comido	escrito
han	amado	comido	escrito

Hello	**Buenos días** _Bwaynohs deeahs_
Good evening	**Buenas tardes/noches** _Bwaynahs tahrdays/nohchays_
Good night	**Buenas noches** _Bwaynahs nohchays_
Goodbye / See you soon	**Hasta la vista / Hasta pronto** _Ahstah lah beestah / Ahstah prohntoh_
Pleased to meet you	**Mucho gusto** _Moochoh goostoh_
How are you?	**¿Cómo está?** _Kohmoh aystah?_
Fine, thank you	**Bien, gracias** _Byayn, grahthyahs_
Please	**Por favor** _Por fahvor_
Excuse me / I'm sorry	**Perdone / Lo siento** _Pehrdohnay / Loh syayntoh_
Yes please/No thanks	**Sí, gracias / No, gracias** _See, grahthyahs/ Noh, grahthyahs_
I would like/We would like...	**Quisiera/Quisiéramos...** _Keesyayrah/Keesyayrahmohs..._

Things to remember

If you want to discover the real Spanish restaurants, remember to choose half board when making your hotel booking.

I'd like to book a single/ double room	**Quisiera reservar una habitación individual / doble** *Keesyayrah rehsayrbahr oonah ahbheetahthyon eendeeveedooahl /dohblay*
I'd like a room with breakfast/half board/ full board	**Quisiera una habitación con desayuno/media pensión /pensión completa** *Keesyayrah oonah ahbheetahthyon kon daysahyoonoh/ maydhyah paynsyon / paynsyon kohmplaytah*
How much is it per night/week?	**¿Cuánto cuesta al día / a la semana?** *Kwahntoh kwaystah ahl deeah / ah lah saymahnah?*
Does the price include breakfast?	**¿El desayuno está comprendido en el precio?** *Ayl daysahyoonoh aystah kohmprayndeedhoh ayn ayl praythyoh?*

We will be staying for three nights from... to...

Nos quedamos por tres noches desde el... hasta el...
Nohs kaydahmohs por trays nohchays daysday ayl... ahstah ayl...

We will arrive at...

Llegaremos a las...
Lyaygahraymohs ah lahs...

We've booked a room in the name of...

Hemos reservado una habitación a nombre de...
Ehmohs rehsehrbahdhoh oonah ahbheetahthyon ah nohmbray day...

Can you have my bags brought up to the room?

¿Pueden llevarme el equipaje a la habitación?
Pwaydhayn lyayvahrmay ayl aykeepahkhay ah lah ahbheetahthyon?

What time is breakfast/ lunch/dinner?

¿A qué hora es el desayuno / la comida / la cena?
¿Ah kay ohrah ays ayl daysahyoonoh/lah kohmeedhah/ lah thaynah?

Can we have breakfast in our room at... o'clock?

¿Nos pueden traer el desayuno a las...?
¿Nohs pwaydhayn trahehr ayl daysahyoonoh ah lahs...?

Can I have my key?

Me puede dar mi llave?
¿May pwaydhay dahr mee lyahvay?

Please, put it on my bill

Póngalo en mi cuenta
Pohngahloh ayn mee kwayntah

I'd like an outside line, please

¿Me puede dar la línea, por favor?
May pwaydhay dahr lah leenayah, por fahvor?

Can I have another blanket/pillow?

¿Me puede dar otra manta / otra almohada?
¿May pwaydhay dahr ohtrah mahntah/ohtrah ahlmohahdhah?

I'm locked out of my room

Me he quedado encerrado fuera de mi habitación
May ay kaydahdhoh aynthehrrahdhoh fwayrah day mee ahbheetahthyon

0	**cero** _thay_roh	14	**catorce** kah_tor_thay
1	**uno** _oon_oh	15	**quince** _keen_thay
2	**dos** dos	16	**dieciséis** dyaythee_says_
3	**tres** trays	17	**diecisiete** dyaythee_syay_tay
4	**cuatro** _kwah_troh	18	**dieciocho** dyaythee_oh_choh
5	**cinco** _theen_koh	19	**diecinueve** dyaythee_nway_vay
6	**seis** says	20	**veinte** _bayn_tay
7	**siete** _syay_tay	21	**veintiuno** bayntee_oon_oh
8	**ocho** _oh_choh	22	**veintidós** bayntee_dhos_
9	**nueve** _nway_vay	23	**veintitrés** bayntee_trays_
10	**diez** dyayth	30	**treinta** _trayn_tah
11	**once** _on_thay	31	**treinta y uno** _trayn_tah ee _oon_oh
12	**doce** _doh_thay	40	**cuarenta** kwah_rayn_tah
13	**trece** _tray_thay	50	**cincuenta** theen_kwayn_tah

60	**sesenta** *say<u>say</u>ntah*	110	**ciento diez** *<u>thyayn</u>toh dyayth*
70	**setenta** *say<u>tay</u>ntah*	200	**doscientos/as** *dos<u>thyayn</u>tohs/ahs*
80	**ochenta** *oh<u>chayn</u>tah*	300	**trescientos/as** *trays<u>thyayn</u>tohs/ahs*
90	**noventa** *noh<u>vayn</u>tah*	1000	**mil** *meel*
100	**cien** *thyayn*	2000	**dos mil** *dos <u>meel</u>*
101	**ciento uno** *<u>thyayn</u>toh <u>oo</u>noh*	1,000,000	**un millón** *oon mee<u>lyon</u>*

1st	**primero** *pree<u>meh</u>roh*	6th	**sexto** *<u>sehks</u>toh*
2nd	**segundo** *say<u>goon</u>doh*	7th	**séptimo** *<u>sehp</u>teemoh*
3rd	**tercero** *tehr<u>thay</u>roh*	8th	**octavo** *ohk<u>tah</u>voh*
4th	**cuarto** *<u>kwahr</u>toh*	9th	**noveno** *noh<u>veh</u>noh*
5th	**quinto** *<u>keen</u>toh*	10th	**décimo** *<u>day</u>theemoh*

Things to remember

> Major credit cards are accepted in virtually all shops,
> hotels, and restaurants in large cities and tourist resorts.
> They are also widely used at filling stations and tollways.

How much is it?	**¿Cuánto cuesta?** *Kwahntoh kwaystah?*
Can I have the bill please?	**¿Puede traerme la cuenta, por favor?** *Pwaydhay trahehrmay lah kwayntah, por fahvor?*
Can I pay by credit card?	**¿Puedo pagar con tarjeta de crédito?** *Pwaydhoh pahkhahr kon tahrkhaytah day kraydheetoh?*
Do you accept checks / traveler's checks?	**¿Aceptan cheques / traveler's cheques?** *Ahthehptahn cheks / travelers cheks?*
Can I have a receipt please?	**¿Me da el recibo, por favor?** *May dah ayl raytheebhoh, por fahvor?*
Is service/VAT included?	**¿Se incluye el servicio / el IVA?** *Say eenklooway ayl sehrbeethyoh / ayl eebah?*

What's the total?

¿Cuánto es todo?
Kwahntoh ays tohdhoh?

Do I have to pay in advance?

¿Tengo que pagar por adelantado?
Tayngoh kay pahgahr por ahdaylahntahdhoh?

Do I have to leave a deposit?

¿Tengo que dejar un adelanto?
Tayngoh kay dehkhahr oon ahdaylahntoh?

I think you have given me the wrong change

Me parece que me ha dado la vuelta equivocada
May pahraythay kay may ah dahdhoh lah bwehltah aykeevohkahdhah

Can you help me, please?   **¿Puede ayudarme, por favor?**
Pwaydhay ahyoodharmay, por fahvor?

What's the matter?   **¿Qué pasa?**
Kay pahsah?

I need help   **Necesito ayuda**
naythayseetoh ahyoodhah

I don't understand   **No entiendo**
Noh ayntyayndoh

Say it again, please   **¿Puede repetir, por favor?**
Pwaydhay raypayteer, por fahvor

I've got no money left   **Me he quedado sin dinero**
May ay kaydahdhoh seen deenayroh

I can't find my son/
daughter   **No encuentro a mi hijo / mi hija**
Noh aynkwayntroh ah mee eekhoh / eekhah

I'm lost   **Me he perdido**
May ay pehrdeedhoh

Leave me alone   **Déjame en paz**
Daykhahmay ayn path

It should firstly be pointed out that the Spanish alphabet has a few extra diacritical letters which contain signs used to indicate different sounds or values of the letter, e.g. **ñ**.

Below is a list giving pronunciation, approximate phonetic symbol and example for each letter. Unless otherwise stated, the pronunciation reads just as if it were English. Whilst the various sounds of the two languages do not correspond exactly, in following these guidelines you should have no difficulty in making yourself understood. Please note that you will occasionally find slight differences to this pattern, particularly in the case of foreign words or diphthongs.

The underlined syllable indicates the stress (or emphasis) on each particular word.

Letter	Pronunciation	Phonetic symbol		Example
Vowels				
a	like **ar** in p**ar**t, but quite short	ah	**carne**	_kahr_nay
e	1] may be like **a** in late	ay	**repollo**	ray_pohl_yoh
	2] occasionally like **e** in get	eh	**pierna**	_pyehr_nah
i	1] like **ee** in m**ee**t	ee	**limón**	lee_mon_
	2] in diphthongs like **y** in yes	y	**quisiera**	kee_syay_rah

o	1] may be similar to **o** in v**o**te	oh **horno**	*ohrnoh*
	2] can be like **o** in g**o**t	o **melón**	*maylon*
u	1] like **oo** in b**oo**t	oo **uvas**	*oovahs*
	2] in diphthongs like **w** in **w**ere	w **cuanto**	*kwahntoh*
y	only a vowel at the end of some words or alone; like **ee** in m**ee**t	ee **muy** y	*mwee*

N.B. **ay** like **igh** in h**igh**   igh   **hay**   *igh*

Consonants

f, k, l, m, n, p, t, x, y   the same as English

b	1] usually as in English	b **besugo**	*baysookhoh*
	2] in between vowels, a sound somewhere between **b** and **v**	bh **caballa**	*kahbhahlyah*
c	1] before **e** and **i** like **th** in **th**ick	th **cebolla**	*thaybohlyah*
	2] in other cases like **k** in **k**ing	k **coco**	*kohkoh*
ch	the same as English	ch **lechuga**	*laychookhah*
d	1] usually as in **d**ark, however less decisive	d **dulce**	*doolthay*

	2] between vowels and at the end of a word, like **th** in **th**is	dh	**hígado**	_ee_chahdhoh
g	1] before **e** and **i** like **ch** in lo**ch**	kh	**gente**	_kh_ayntay
	2] In other cases, generally like **g** in **g**o	g	**langosta**	lahn_goh_stah
h	always silent		**huevos**	_way_vohs
j	like **ch** in lo**ch**	kh	**jámon**	khah_mon_
ll	like **lli** in mi**lli**on	ly	**ajillo**	ah_kheel_yoh
ñ	like **ni** in o**ni**on	ni	**coñac**	coh_niahk_
qu	like **k** in **k**it	k	**queso**	_kay_soh
r	a more emphatic trill, particularly with **rr** or at the start of a word	r	**rosa**	_ro_sah
s	like the **s** in **s**it, but often with a slight lisp	s	**pastas**	_pah_stahs
v	1] usually like **b** in **b**ig, but not so tense	b	**venado**	bay_nah_dhoh
	2] in between vowels it resembles an English **v**	v	**favor**	fah_vor_
z	like **th** in **th**ick	th	**maíz**	mah_eeth_

New Year's Eve

Nochevieja
Nohchaybyaykhah

Good Friday

Viernes Santo
Byayrnays Sahntoh

Easter

Semana Santa
Saymahnah Sahntah

Christmas Eve

Noche buena
Nohchay bwaynah

Christmas

Navidad
Nahbeedhadh

Maundy Thursday

Jueves Santo
Khwayvays Sahntoh

Feast of the Immaculate
Conception

Inmaculada
Eenmahkoolahdhah

Is it far?

¿Está lejos?
Aystah lehkhos?

Is it expensive?

¿Cuesta mucho?
kwaystah moochoh?

Can you help me?

¿Puede ayudarme?
Pwaydhay ahyoodharmay?

Have you understood?

¿Ha entendido?
Ah ayntayndeedhoh?

Where are the shops?

¿Dónde están las tiendas?
Dohnday aystahn lahs tyayndahs?

How do I get there?

¿Cómo se llega allí?
Kohmoh say lyaygah ahlyee?

What is this?

¿Qué es esto?
Kay ays aystoh?

Where is the restroom please?

¿Dónde está el baño, por favor?
Dohnday aystah ayl bahnioh, por fahvor?

Do you have to pay for the toilets?

¿El servicio del baño se paga?
Ayl sehrbeethyoh dayl bahnioh say pahgah?

There's no toilet paper/soap

No hay papel higiénico / jabón
Noh igh pahpehl eekhyayneekoh / khahbhon

Is there a toilet for the disabled?

¿Hay un baño para minusválidos?
Igh oon bahnioh pahrah meenoosbahleedhohs?

The toilet is blocked

El baño está obstruido
Ayl bahnioh aystah ohbstrooeedhoh

Things to remember

> Smoking in public places (museums, cinemas, etc.) and on public transport (buses, subways, etc.) is forbidden throughout Spain. Trains have special smoking compartments. In most restaurants there are no restrictions.

Is smoking allowed here? | **¿Se puede fumar aquí?**
Say pwaydhay foomahr ahkee?

Do you mind if I smoke? | **¿Le molesta si fumo?**
Lay mohlaystah see foomoh?

Could I have an ashtray? | **¿Dónde hay un cenicero?**
Dohnday igh oon thayneethayroh?

Do you have matches? | **¿Tienen / teneis cerillas?**
Tyaynayn/ taynays thehreelyahs?

Have you got a light? | **¿Tiene fuego?**
Tyaynay fwaygoh?

Would you mind not smoking? | **¿Le importaría dejar de fumar?**
Lay eempohrtahreeah dehkhahr day foomahr?

Things to remember

All cities have authorized taxi firms that generally have white vehicles with a red stripe, although in Barcelona they are yellow and black. You are advised to avoid "private" taxis, but if left with no choice, make sure you agree on a price before setting off.

Can you call me a taxi please?	**¿Puede llamarme a un taxi, por favor?** *Pwaydhay lyáhmahrmay ah oon tahksee, por fahvor?*
To the main station/the airport	**A la estación central/al aeropuerto** *Ah lah aystahthyon thayntrahl/ahl ahayrohpwayrtoh*
Take me to this address/ this hotel	**Lléveme a esta dirección/a este hotel** *Lyayvaymay ah aystah deerehkthyon/ ah ayslay ohtayl*
Is it far?	**¿Está lejos?** *Aystah lehklos?*
I'm in a hurry	**Tengo mucha prisa** *Tayngoh moochah preesah*
How much will it cost?	**¿Cuánto me costará?** *Kwahntoh may kohstahrah?*
Stop here/on the corner	**Párese aquí / en la esquina** *Pahraysay ahkee/ayn lah ayskeenah*
How much is it?	**¿Cuánto es?** *Kwahntoh ays?*

Things to remember

Most public telephones take 100, 50, or 25-peseta coins, although cardphones are now commonplace. Phonecards can be purchased from tobacconists, newsstands, and special vending machines.

Is there a phone?

¿Hay un teléfono?
Igh oon taylayfohnoh?

I'd like an outside line

¿Me pone línea?
May pohnay leenayah?

Can I have a 500/1000-peseta phonecard?

Déme una tarjeta telefónica de 500/1000 pesetas
Daymay oonah tahrkhaytah taylayfohneekah day keenyayntohs/meel paysaytahs

I'd like to make a phone call

Quisiera llamar por teléfono
Keesyayrah lyahmahr por taylayfohnoh

The number is... extension...

El número es... interno...
Ayl noomayroh ays... eentayrnoh...

How much is it to phone the United States, England...?

¿Cuánto cuesta llamar a Estados Unidos, Inglaterra...?
Kwahntoh kwaystah lyahmahr ah Aystahdhohs Ooneedhohs, Eenglahtehrrah...

I can't get through

No consígo que me den linea
Noh konh<u>see</u>goh kay may dayn <u>lee</u>nayah

What's the code for...

¿Cuál es el prefijo de...
Kwahl ays ayl pray<u>fee</u>khoh day...

Hello, this is...

Soy...
Soy...

Can I speak to...?

¿Puedo hablar con...?
<u>Pway</u>dhoh ah<u>blahr</u> kon...?

Could you give me some change in 25/50/100-peseta coins?

¿Puede cambiármelos en monedas de 25 / 50 / 100 pesetas?
<u>Pway</u>dhay kahm<u>byahr</u>maylohs ayn moh<u>nay</u>dahs day bayntee<u>theen</u>koh/ theen<u>kwayn</u>tah/ thyayn pay<u>say</u>tahs

It's busy

Comunica
Kohmoo<u>nee</u>kah

I've been cut off

Me han cortado la llamada / la comunicación
May ahn kohr<u>tah</u>dhoh lah lyah<u>mah</u>dhah/lah kohmooneekah<u>thyon</u>

It's a bad line

No se oye bien
Noh say <u>oy</u>ay byayn

I'm sorry, wrong number

Perdone, me he equivocado de número
Pehr<u>doh</u>nay, may ay aykeevoh<u>kah</u>dhoh day <u>noo</u>mayroh

YOU MAY HEAR: ─────────────────────────

Hello, who's speaking? **¿Diga, quién es?**
Deegah, kyayn ays?

Hold the line **Permanezaca en línea**
Permanézhca ayn leenayah

Please try again later **Inténtelo más tarde, por favor**
Eentayntayloh mahs tahrday, por fahvor

He/she is not here **No está**
Noh aystah

You've got the wrong number **Se ha equivocado de número**
Say ah aykeevohkahdhoh day noomayroh

What time is it?	¿Qué hora es?	*Kay ohrah ays?*
It's...	Son las...	*Son lahs...*
x : 05	... y cinco	*... ee theenkoh*
x : 10	... y diez	*... ee dyayth*
x : 15	... y cuarto	*... ee kwahrtoh*
x : 20	... y veinte	*... ee bayntay*
x : 30	... y media	*... ee maydhyah*
x : 40	... menos veinte	*... maynohs bayntay*
x : 45	... menos cuarto	*... maynohs kwahrtoh*

Eight A.M./P.M.	**Las ocho de la mañana/de la tarde** *Lahs ohchoh day lah mahniahnah/day lah tahrday*
Midday	**Mediodía** *maydhyohdheeah*
Midnight	**Las doce de la noche** *Lahs dohthay day lah nohchay*

What time do you (does it) open/close?	**¿A qué hora abre / cierra ?** *Ah kay ohrah ahbray /thyehrrah?*
What time does the restaurant close?	**¿A qué hora cierra el restaurante?** *Ah kay ohrah thyehrrah ayl raystowrahntay?*
What time do the shops close?	**¿A qué hora cierran las tiendas?** *Ah kay ohrah thyayrrahn lahs tyayndahs?*
How long will it take to get there?	**¿Cuánto se tardará en llegar?** *Kwahntoh say tahrdahrah ayn lyaykhahr ?*
We arrived early/late	**Hemos llegado pronto / tarde** *Ehmohs lyaykhahdhoh prohntoh / tahrday*
It's early/late	**Es pronto / tarde** *Ays prohntoh/ tahrday*
The table is booked for... this evening	**La mesa está reservada para las... de esta noche** *Lah maysah aystah rehsayrbahdah pahrah lahs... day aystah nohchay*

Things to remember

As one might expect, it is common practice to tip in hotels, the restaurant waiter, taxi driver, junior hairdresser, etc. The customary amount is between 5 and 10% which in most cases should work out a few hundred pesetas.

I'm sorry, I don't have change
Lo siento, no tengo suelto
Loh syayntoh, noh tayngoh swayltoh

Keep the change
Tenga, la vuelta
Tayngah, lah bwehltah

Can you give me... in change
¿Me puede dar... en monedas?
May pwaydhay dahr... ayn mohnaydahs?

Is the tip included?
¿Está incluida la propina?
Aystah eenklooeedhah lah prohpeenah?

Take ... pesetas
Cobre... pesetas
Kohbray... paysaytahs

Half a liter of...

Medio litro de...
Maydhyoh leetroh day...

A liter of...

Un litro de...
Oon leetroh day...

A kilo of...

Un quilo de...
Oon keeloh day...

Half a kilo of...

Medio quilo de...
Maydhyoh keeloh day...

100 grams of...

100 gramos de...
thyayn grahmohs day...

A slice of...

Un trozo de...
Oon trohthoh day...

A portion of...

Una porción / ración de...
Oonah porthyon/rahthyon day...

A dozen...

Una docena de...
Oonah dothehnah day...

Two hundred pesetas' worth of...

Doscientas pesetas de...
Dosthyayntahs paysaytahs day...

GASTRONOMIC DICTIONARY

a lot mucho _moochoh_

able, to be poder _pohdhayr_

above encima _aynthymah_

account cuenta _kwayntah_

ache mal/dolor _mahl/dohlor_

acid ácido _ahtheedhoh_

additive aditivo _ahdeeteevoh_

address dirección _deeraykthyon_

adult adulto _ahdhooltoh_

after después _dayspways_

against contra _kohntrah_

air aire _ighray_

air-conditioning aire acondicionado _ighray ahkondeethyohnahdhoh_

airplane avión _ahvyon_

airport aeropuerto _ahayrohpwayrtoh_

alcoholic alcohólico _ahlkohohleekoh_

alcoholic drinks alcohólicos _ahlkohohleekohs_

alert atento _ahtayntoh_

all todo _tohdhoh_

allergy alergia _ahlehrkhyah_

almonds almendras _ahlmayndrahs_

almost casi _kahsee_

also también _tahmbyayn_

always siempre _seeaympray_

amongst entre _ayntray_

anchovy anchoa _ahnchohah_

angle ángulo _ahngooloh_

announcement comunicación _kohmooneekahthyon_

antibiotic antibiótico _ahnteebyohteekoh_

any cualquier/a _kwahlkyehr/ah_

anything algo _ahlgoh_

aperitif aperitivo _ahpayreeteevoh_

appetite apetito _ahpayteetoh_

appetizer entremés _ayntraymays_

apple manzana _mahnthahnah_

appointment cita _theetah_

appreciate aceptar con agrado _athayptahr kon agrahdhoh_

apricot albaricoque _ahlbahreekohkay_

April abril _ahbreel_

aroma aroma _ahrohmah_

aromatic aromático _ahrohmahteekoh_

aromatic herbs especias
ayspaythyahs

around alrededor
ahlraydhaydhohr

arrive, to llegar *lyaygahr*

artichoke alcachofa
ahlkahchohfah

as como *kohmoh*

as far as hasta *ahstah*

ash ceniza *thayneethah*

ashtray cenicero
thayneethayroh

ask, to pedir/ preguntar
pehdheer / praygoontahr

asparagus espárragos
ayspahpahrrahgohs

aspirin aspirina
ahspeereenah

at least al menos *ahl
maynohs*

at once enseguida
aynsaygweedah

attentive atento *ahtayntoh*

August agosto *ahgohstoh*

authentic auténtico
owtaynteekoh

avocado aguacate
ahgwahkahtay

avoid, to evitar *aybeetahr*

baby carriage carroza de
niños *carrothah day
neeniohs*

baby food homogeneizado
ohmohkhaynaythadhoh

backwards detrás *daytrahs*

bacon, smoky bacon
ahumado *baykon
ahoomahdhoh*

bad feo *fehoh*; **bad** mal/o
mahl/mahloh

bag bolso *bolsoh*

baking coción *cothyon*

banana plátano *plahtahnoh*

Band Aid tirita *teereetah*

bank banco *bahnkoh*

bar bar *bar*; **bar** local
lohkahl

barbecue, to cocer a la
brasa *kothayr ah lah
brahsah*

barley cebada
thaybahdhah

barman camarero del bar
kahmahrayroh dayl bahr

basil albahaca
ahlbhahahkah

bass (fish) lubina
loobheenah

beans alubias
ahloobheeahs

beat, to batir *bahteer*

because porque *porkay*

beef novillo *nohbeelyoh*;
bovino *bohbheenoh*

beer cerveza *thehrbaythah*;
bitter c. oscura *th.
skoorah*; **lager,** c. clara *th.
klahrah*; **large beer,** c.
grande *th. grahnday*; **small
beer** c. pequeña *th.
paykayniah*; **draught beer**
caña *kahniah*

beet, beetroot remolacha
raymohlahchah

before antes *ahntays*

begin, to comenzar
kohmaynthahr

behind detrás *daytrahs*

bell pepper pimiento
peemyayntoh

beside junto a.. *goontoh ah*

best mejor *mehkhor*

better mejor *mehkhor*

between entre *ayntray*

big grande *grahnday*

bill cuenta *kwayntah*

biscuits biscotes/ galletas
beeskohtays/gahlyaytahs

bitter amargo *ahmahrgoh*;
bitter áspero *ahspayroh*

bitter liqueur licor *leekor*

black negro *nehgroh*

blend mezcla *maythklah*

boil, to hervir *ehrbheer*

boiled cocido *kotheedhoh*

bone hueso *waysoh*

book libro *leebroh*

book, to reservar
rehsayrbahr

booked reservado
rehsehrbahdhoh

booking reserva *rehsayrbah*

bottle opener abrebotellas
ahbraybohtaylyahs

bottle botella *bohtaylyah*

bottled embotellado
aymbohtaylyahdhoh

box caja *kahkhah*

boy chico *cheekoh*

brain cerebro *thayraybroh*

brandy aguardiente
ahgwahrdyayntay

bread pan *pahn*

breadsticks palitos de pan
pahleetohs day pahn

breadcrumbs pan rallado
pahn rahlyahdhoh

breaded empanado
aympaynahdhoh

break, to romper *rohmpayr*

breakdown estropeado/
destrozo *aystrohpayahdhoh/
daystrohthoh*

breakfast desayuno
daysahyoonoh

bream, gilthead dorada
dohrahdoh

breast pecho *paychoh*

bring, to traer/llevar
trah<u>ehr</u>/lyay<u>var</u>

broad beans habas
<u>ah</u>bhahs

broccoli bréjoles
<u>bray</u>khohlays

broken
estropeado/destrozo/roto
*aystrohpay<u>ah</u>dhoh/
day<u>stroh</u>thoh/<u>roh</u>toh*

broth caldo *<u>kahl</u>dhoh*

browned dorado
doh<u>rah</u>dhoh; sofrito
sohf<u>ree</u>toh

brush cepillo *thay<u>pee</u>lyoh*

Brussels sprout repollo de
Bruselas *ray<u>poh</u>lyoh day
broo<u>say</u>lahs*

burn, to quemar *kay<u>mahr</u>*

burnt quemado
kay<u>mah</u>dhoh

bus autobús *owtohb<u>hoos</u>*

busy ocupado
ohkoo<u>pah</u>dhoh

butcher's carnicería
kahrneethay<u>ree</u>ah

butter mantequilla
mahntay<u>kee</u>lyah

buttered con mantequilla
kon mahntay<u>kee</u>lyah

button botón *boh<u>ton</u>*

buy, to comprar *kohm<u>prahr</u>*

cabbage berza *<u>behr</u>tha*;
repollo *ray<u>poh</u>lyoh*

cake pastel *pahs<u>tayl</u>*;
tarta *<u>tahr</u>tah*

call up (telephone) llamada
por teléfono *lyah<u>mah</u>dhah
por tay<u>lay</u>fohnoh*

call, long-distance
interurbana
eentayroor<u>bah</u>nah

call, to llamar *lyah<u>mahr</u>*

calm tranquilo *tran<u>kee</u>loh*

calories calorías
kahloh<u>ree</u>ahs

camomile camomila
kahmoh<u>mee</u>lah

can lata *<u>lah</u>tah*

can; be able, to poder
pohd<u>hayr</u>

cancel, to anular
ahnoo<u>lahr</u>; cancelar
kahnthay<u>lahr</u>

candies dulces *<u>dool</u>thays*

candle vela *<u>bay</u>lah*

candy caramelo
kahrah<u>may</u>loh

canned meat carne en lata
<u>kahr</u>nay ayn <u>lah</u>tah

can-opener abrelatas
ahbray<u>lah</u>tahs

cap, bottle tapón de la
botella *tah<u>pon</u> day lah
boh<u>tay</u>lyah*

capers alcaparras
ahlkahpahrrahs

capon gallo capado
gahlyoh kahpahdhoh

car park aparcamiento
ahpahrkahmyayntoh

cardoons cardos *kahrdohs*

caretaker guarda *gwahrdah*

carrot zanahoria
thahnahohryah

carry, to traer/llevar
trahehr/lyayvar

cash desk caja *kahkhah*

cash contado *kohntahdhoh*

cashier cajera *cakhayrah*

casserole dish cazuela
kahthwaylah

cauliflower coliflor
koleeflor

celery apio *ahpyoh*

center centro *thayntroh*

central central *thayntrahl*

cereals cereales
thayrayahlays

chair silla *seelyah*

champagne champán
shahmpahn

change resto *raystoh*

change (small)
monedas/dinero suelto
*mohnaydahs/ deenayroh
swayltoh*

change, keep the Tenga, la
vuelta *Tayngah, lah
bwehltah*

change, to cambiar
kahmbyahr

charge, to; debit, to cargar
en cuenta *kahrgahr ayn
kwayntah*

cheap barato *bahrahtoh*

check cheque *chaykay*

check, to controlar
kohntrohlahr

checkout caja *kahkhah*

cheese queso *kaysoh*

cherry cereza *thayraythah*

chestnut castaña
kahstahniah; marrón
mahrrohn

chew, to masticar
mahsteekahr

chicken pollo *pohlyoh*

chick-peas garbanzos
gahrbahnthohs

chicory achicoria
ahcheekohreeah

child niño *neenioh*

chili pepper guindilla
geendeelyah

chocolate chocolate
chohkohlahtay

chocolate, hot chocolate
líquido *chohkohlahtay
leekeedhoh*

chocolates chocolatinas *chohkohlah<u>tee</u>nahs;* bombones *bohm<u>boh</u>nays*

chop chuleta *choo<u>lay</u>tah*

chop, to triturar *treetoo<u>rahr</u>*

chopped triturado *treetoo<u>rah</u>dhoh*

Christmas Navidad *Nahbee<u>dhadh</u>*

cigar puro *<u>poo</u>roh*

cigarette cigarrillo *theekhahr<u>ree</u>lyoh*

cinnamon canela *kah<u>nay</u>lah*

citrus fruits los agrios *los <u>ah</u>khryohs*

city ciudad *thyoo<u>dhahdh</u>*

clams almejas *ahl<u>meh</u>khahs*

clams (small) chirlas *<u>cheer</u>lahs*

clean limpio *<u>leem</u>pyoh*

clear claro *<u>klah</u>roh*

client cliente *klee<u>ayn</u>tay*

climb, to subir *soob<u>heer</u>*

cloakroom guardarropa *khwahrdahr<u>roh</u>pah*

clock reloj *reh<u>lokh</u>*

close, to cerrar *thehr<u>rahr</u>*

closed cerrado *thehr<u>rah</u>dhoh*

closure cierre *<u>thyehr</u>ray*

coals brasa *<u>brah</u>sah*

coat abrigo *ah<u>bree</u>goh*

cockerel gallo pequeño *<u>gah</u>lyoh pay<u>kay</u>nioh*

cocoa cacao *kah<u>kow</u>*

coconut (nueces de) coco *(<u>nway</u>thays day) <u>koh</u>koh*

coffee café *kah<u>fay</u>;* **black coffee** café solo *kah<u>fay</u> <u>soh</u>loh;* **coffee with milk** café con leche *kah<u>fay</u> kon <u>lay</u>chay;* **decaffeinated coffee** café descafeinado *kah<u>fay</u> dayskahfayee<u>nah</u>doh;* **espresso coffee** café expreso *kah<u>fay</u> exs<u>pray</u>soh*

coin moneda *moh<u>nay</u>dah*

cold frío *<u>free</u>oh*

color color *koh<u>lor</u>*

coloring agents colorantes *kohlo<u>rahn</u>tays*

come back, to volver *vohl<u>bayr</u>*

come out, to salir *sah<u>leer</u>*

come, to venir *bay<u>neer</u>*

comfortable cómodo *<u>koh</u>mohdoh*

communication comunicación *kohmooneekah<u>thyon</u>*

complaint reclamación *rayklahmah<u>thyon</u>*

complete integral
eentaygrahl

compulsory obligatorio
ohbhleegahtohryoh

cone cono *kohnoh*

confirm, to confirmar
kohnfeermahr

contact lenses lentillas
laynteelyahs

continue, to continuar
conteenooahr

control, to controlar
kohntrohlahr

convenient cómodo
kohmohdoh

cook cocinero
kohtheenayroh

cook, to cocer *kohthayr*

cooked cocido *kotheedhoh*

cooking coción *cothyon*;
cocina *kohtheenah*

cool fresco *frehskoh*

cool, to enfriar *aynfreeahr*

cork tapón de la botella
tahpon day lah bohtaylyah

corn maíz *maeeth*

corner ángulo *ahngooloh*;
esquina *ayskeenah*

corn-on-the-cob mazorca
mahthohrkah

cost coste *kohstay*

cost, to costar *kohstahr*

cotton algodón
ahlkhohdon

country país *payees*

countryside campo
kahmpoh

country-style rústico
roosteekoh

course plato *plahtoh*

course, main manjar
mahnkhahr

cover charge cubierto
koobyehrtoh

cover cubierto
koobyehrtoh

cover, to cubrir *koobreer*

crab cangrejo
kahngrehkhoh

cream crema *kraymah*

cream/single/whipped
nata/líquida/montada
*nahtah/leekweedhah/
mohntahdhah*

credit card tarjeta de
crédito *tahrkhaytah day
kraydheetoh*

crêpe oreja de abad
oraykha day ahbahd

crisp crujiente
krookhyayntay

croissant media luna
maydheeah loonah

croquettes croquetas
krochaytahs

croutons tostadas
 tohstahdhohs
crowded lleno de gente
 lyaynoh day khayntay
crunchy crujiente
 krookhyayntay
crystal cristal *kreestahl*
cube (ice-cube) cubito (de
 hielo) *koobheetoh (day
 yayloh)*
cucumber pepino
 paypeenoh
cuisine cocina *kohtheenah*
cup, ice-cream copa
 kohpah
cup/(small) coffee cup
 taza/tacita *tahthah/tathita*
currency divisa *deebeesah*
cushion
 almohada/almohadilla
 *ahlmohahdhah/
 ahlmohahdheelyah*
customer cliente
 kleeayntay
cut, to cortar *kohrtahr*
cutlery cubiertos
 koobyehrtohs
cuttlefish sepias *saypyahs*

dance, to bailar *bighlahr*
dark oscuro *ohskooroh*
date (meeting) cita *theetah*

dates (fruit) dátiles
 dahteelays
day día *deeah*
December diciembre
 deethyaymbray
decorated decorado
 daykohrahdhoh
decoration decoración
 daykohrahthyon
delay retraso *raytrahsoh*
demand pregunta/petición
 praygoontah/payteethyohn
dentures dentadura postiza
 *dayntahdhoorah
 pohsteethah*
depart, to irse *eersay*
deposit, to depositar
 daypohseetahr
dessert postre *pohstray*
diabetic diabético
 deeahbayteekoh
diet alimentación
 ahleemayntahthyon
diet (slimming) dieta
 deeaytah
different distinto
 deesteentoh
difficult difícil *deefeetheel*
digestible digerible
 deekhayreeblay
digestive digestivo
 deekhaysteeboh

dinner cena *thaynah*
direction dirección
 deerehkthyon
directions indicaciones
 eendeekahthyonays
dirty sucio *soothyoh*
disabled minusválido
 meenoosbahleedhoh
discothèque discoteca
 deeskohtaykah
dish plato *plahtoh*
dish, sundae copa *kohpah*
disinfect desinfectar
 dayseenfayktahr
disinfectant desinfectante
 dayseenfayktahntay
distance distancia
 deestahnthyah
distributor distribuidor
 deestreebweedohr
disturb, to molestar
 mohlaystahr
do, to hacer *ahthehr*
doctor médico
 mehdheekoh
documents documentos
 dokoomayntohs
dollars dólares *dohlahrays*
door puerta *pwayrtah*
double doble *dohblay*
down abajo *ahbhahkhoh*
drink bebida *baybheedah*

drink, to beber *baybhayr*
dry seco *saykoh*
drumstick muslo de pollo
 moosloh day pohlyoh
duck pato *pahtoh*
dummy chupete
 choopaytay

each cada *kahdhah*
earring pendiente
 payndyayntay
Easter Semana Santa
 Saymahnah Sahntah
easy fácil *fahtheel*
eat, to comer *kohmehr*
economical barato
 bahrahtoh
EEC CEE *thay ay ay*
eel anguila *ahngweelah*
egg huevo *wayvoh*; **boiled
 eggs** huevos duros
 wayvohs doorohs; **eggs
 fried in butter** huevos con
 mantequilla *wayvohs kon
 mahntaykeelyah*;
 scrambled eggs huevos
 revueltos *wayvohs
 raybwehltohs*
eggplant berenjena
 bayraynkhaynah
eggwhite clara de huevo
 klahrah day wayvoh

elevator ascensor *ahsthaynsohr*
embassy embajada *aymbahkhahdhah*
empty vacío *bahthyoh*
enclosed incluido *eenklooeedhoh*
end fin *feen*
endive endivia *ayndeebheeah*
end-of-the-line (bus, etc.) terminal de parada *tehrmeenahl day pahrahdhah*
England Inglaterra *Eenglahtehrrah*
English inglés *eenglays*
enjoy, to degustar *daygoostahr*
enough bastante *bahstahntay*
enough, to be bastar *bahstahr*
enter, to entrar *ayntrahr*
entrance, entry entrada *ayntradhah*
envelope sobre *sohbray*
equal igual *eekwahll*
error error *ayrrohr*
evening tarde noche *tahrday nohchay*
evening, this esta noche *aystah nohchay*

every cada *kahdhah*
evil mal/o *mahl/mahloh*
except excepto *exthayptoh*
exchange rate cambio *kahmbyoh*
excursion excursión *exkoorsyon*
exit salida *sahleedhah*
expense compra *kohmprah*
expensive caro *kahroh*
experienced experto *expayrtoh*
expert experto *expayrtoh*
extension, (telephone) interno *eentayrnoh*
external externo *extayrnoh*
extract extracto *extrahkhtoh*
eye ojo *ohkhoh*

fainted desvanecido *desvanezhido*
fall, to caerse *kahayrsay*
familiar familiar *fahmeelyahr*
family (adj.) familiar *fahmeelyahr*
family familia *fahmeelyah*
famous famoso *fahmohsoh*
fancy cake pasta (dulce) *pahstah (doolthay)*
far lejos *lehkhos*

fast rápido _rahpeedhoh_

fat graso/gordo
grahsoh/gohrdhoh

favor favor _fah**vor**_

February febrero
fehbrehroh

feet/on foot pie/a pie
pyay/ah pyay

fennel hinojo _eenohkhoh_

few, a algunos _ahl**goo**nohs_;
poco _**poh**koh_

field campo _**kahm**poh_

fig higo _**ee**goh_

filled relleno _ray**lyay**noh_

fillet filete _fee**lay**tay_

filling relleno _ray**lyay**noh_

filter, to filtrar _fee**ltrahr**_

find, to encontrar
aynkohn**trahr**

fine sutil _soo**teel**_

finish, to terminar
tehrmee**nahr**

fire fuego _**fway**goh_

fish pescado/pez
pays**kahd**hoh/ pehth

fizzy espumoso/con mucho
gas _ayspoo**moh**soh/kon
moochoh gas_

flame llama _lyah**mah**_

flask (straw-covered)
botella _boh**tay**lyah_

flavor gusto _**goo**stoh_;
sabor _sah**bhohr**_

flavor, to saborear
sahbhohray**ahr**

flavoring sazón _sah**thon**_

flesh pulpa _**pool**pah_

flight vuelo _**bway**loh_

floor (story) piso _**pee**soh_

flour harina _ah**reenah**_

flowers flores _floh**rays**_

fly mosca _**mohs**kah_

for por/para _por/ pahrah_

foreign extranjero
extrahn**khay**roh

foreigner extranjero
extrahn**khay**roh

forget, to olvidar
ohlbee**dhahr**

fork tenedor _taynay**dhohr**_

forward adelante
ahday**lahn**tay

fourth cuarto _**kwahr**toh_

fragrance aroma _ah**rohmah**_

France Francia _frahn**thyah**_

free gratis _**grah**tees_; libre
**lee**bray

French francés _fran**zhès**_

French beans judías verdes
khoo**dhee**ahs **hol**uays

French fries patatas fritas
pah**tah**tahs **free**tahs

fresh fresco _**freh**skoh_

Friday viernes _byayrnays_
fried food fritura _freetoorah_
fried/mixed fry frito/fritura mixta _freetoh/freetoorah meextah_
friend amigo _ahmeegoh_
front, in delante _daylahntay_
frozen congelado _kohnkhaylahdhoh_
fruit juice, freshly squeezed zumo natural _thoomoh nahtoorahl_
fruit salad macedonia _mahthaydohnyah_
fruit/fresh/dried fruta/fresca/seca _frootah/frehskah/saykah_
frying pan sartén _sahrtayn_
fry-up fritura _freetoorah_
full lleno _lyaynoh_
full-bodied corposo _kohrpohsoh_

game (pheasant, etc.) caza _kahthah_
garden jardín _khahrdeen_
garlic ajo _ahkhoh_
garnish guarnición _gwahrneethyon_
gelatine gelatina _khaylahteenah_

gender género _khaynayroh_
genuine auténtico _owtaynteekoh_
Germany Alemania _Ahlaymahnyah_
get on, to subir _soobheer_
gherkins pepinillos _paypeeneelyohs_
giblets asaduras _ahsahdoorahs_
girl chica _cheekah_
give, to dar _dahr_
glass cristal _kreestahl_
glass/liqueur glass vaso / v. pequeño _bahsoh / b. paykaynioh_
glasses gafas _gahfahs_
gloves guantes _gwahntays_
go, to ir _eer_
go back, to volver _vohlbayr_
go out, to salir _sahleer_
go up, to subir _soobheer_
gold oro _ohroh_
golden brown dorado _dohrahdhoh_
good bien _byayn;_ bueno _bwaynoh_
goose oca _ohkah_
gourd calabaza _kahlahbhathah_
grain grano _grahnoh_

grapefruit pomelo
pohmayloh
grapes uvas *oovahs*
grated rallado *rahlyahdhoh*
gratin, (au) gratinado
grahteenahdhoh
gravy guiso *gweesoh*
greasy untado/grasiento
oontahdhoh/grahsyayntoh
great grande *grahnday*
Great Britain Gran Bretaña
Grahn Braytahniah
green verde *behrday*
grill parrilla *pahrreelyah*
group grupo *groopoh*;
pandilla *pahndeelyah*
guard guaɩda *gwahrdah*
guide guía *gweeah*
Guinea fowl gallina de
Guinea *gahlyeenah day
Geenayah*

hake merluza *mayrloothah*
half mitad/medio
meetahdh/maydhyoh
hall sala *sahlah*
ham jamón *khahmon*
hand mano *mahnoh*
handbag bolso pequeño
bolsoh paykaynioh
happen, to suceder
soothaydayr

happened, what (has) qué
ha pasado *kay ah
pahsahdhoh*
happy contento
kohntayntoh
hard duro *dooroh*
hare liebre *lyehbray*
harmless inocuo *eenokwoh*
hat sombrero *sohmbrayroh*
have a good meal! ¡qué
aproveche! *kay
ahprohbaychay*
have to, to deber *daybhayr*
hazelnuts avellanas
ahvaylyahnahs
headache dolor de cabeza
dohlor day kahbhaythah
hear, to oír *oheer*
heat, to calentar
kahlayntahr
heating calefacción
kahlayfahkthyon
heavy pesado *paysahdhoh*
hello (answering phone)
diga *deegah*
help, to ayudar *ahyoodhar*
hen gallina *gahlynah*
herb tea tisana *teesahnah*
herbs, aromatic hierbas
aromáticas *yehrbahs
ahrohmahteekahs*
here aquí *ahkee*

herring arenque *ahrehnkay*
high chair silla para bebés *seelyah pahrah baybays*
hire, to alquilar *ahlkeelahr*
hold, to tener *taynayr*
holiday, public fiesta *fyaystah*
holidays vacaciones *bahkahthyohnays*
honey miel *myehl*
hors-d'oeuvres entremés *ayntraymays*
hospital hospital *ohspeetahl*
hot caliente *kahlyayntay*
hot (spicy) picante *peekahntay*
hotel hotel *ohtayl*
hour hora *ohrah*
how como *kohmoh*
how many cuantos *kwahntohs*
how much cuanto *kwahntoh*
hundred cien/to *thyayn/toh*
hunger hambre *ahmbray*
hurry prisa *preesah*
hurry, to be in a tener prisa *taynayr preesah*
hurry, to do something in a apresurarse *ahpraysoorahrsay*

husband marido *mahreedhoh*

ice hielo *yayloh,*
ice-cream helado *aylahdhoh*
ice-cream shop (parlor) heladería *aylahdhayreeah*
identity card carnet de identidad *kahrnay day eedaynteedhad*
ill enfermo *aynfehrmoh*
important importante *eempohrtahntay*
impossible imposible *eempohseebhlay*
in cash al contado *ahl kohntahdhoh*
in order to por/para *pohr/pahrah*
included, inclusive incluído *eenklooeedhoh*; comprendido *kohmprayndeedhoh*
inconvenient incómodo *eenkohmohdhoh*
indoors al cubierto *ahl koobyehrtoh*
inexpensive barato *bahrahtoh*
inform, to advertir *ahdbehrteer*; informar *eenformahr*

information informaciones *eenformahthyonays*
inn tasca *tahskah*
insect insecto *eensehktoh*
inside dentro de *dayntroh day*; interno *eentayrnoh*
instead en cambio *ayn kahmbyoh*
internal interno *eentayrnoh*
invite, to invitar *eenbeetahr*
invoice factura *fahktoorah*
Ireland Irlanda *Eerlahndah*
Italy Italia *Eetahlyah*

jacket chaqueta *chahkaytah*
jam confitura *kohnfeetoorah*; mermelada *mayrmaylahdah*
January enero *aynayroh*
jelly gelatina *khaylahteenah*
jug jarra *khahrrah*
juice zumo *thoomoh*
July julio *khoolyoh*
June junio *khoonyoh*
just propio *prohpyoh*

keep, to custodiar/cuidar *koostohdyar/kweedahr*; tener *taynayr*
keeper guarda *gwahrdah*

kid (young goat) cabra pequeña *kahbrah paykayniah*
kidney riñón *reeniohn*
kind (type) género *khaynayroh*
kitchen cocina *kohtheenah*
knife cuchillo *koocheelyoh*
know, to saber *sahbhayr*

label etiqueta *ayteekaytah*
lady señora *sayniohrah*
lager c. clara *c. klahrah*
lake lago *laghoh*
lamb carnero *kahrnayroh*
lamb cordero *kohrdayroh*
lard manteca de cerdo *mahntaykah day thehrdoh*
lard tocino *tohtheenoh*
large grande *grahnday*
last último *oolteemoh*
lean delgado/sin grasa *daylhahdhoh/seen grahsah*
leave, to dejar *dehkhahr*; irse *eersay*
leave, to salir *sahleer*
leeks puerros *pwayrrohs*
left, to be quedar/se *kaydahr/say*
leg pierna *pyehrnah*
lemon limón *leemon*

lemonade limonada
leemohnahdah
lens lente *layntay*
lentils lentejas *layntaykhas*
less menos *maynohs*
lettuce lechuga *laychoogah*
lift ascensor *ahsthaynsohr*
light ligero *leekhayroh*
light luz *looth*
light, to encender
aynthayndhayr
like como *kohmoh*
line hilo *eeloh*
line (telephone) línea
leenayah
liqueur licor *leekor*
list lista *leestah*
lit encendido
aynthayndeedhoh
liter litro *leetroh*
little poco *pohkoh*
liver/livers hígado/
higaditos *eekhahdhoh/
eekhadheetohs*
lobster langosta
lahngohstah
lobster (baby) langostino
lahngohsteenoh
local local *lohkahl*
loin lomo *lohmoh*
long largo *lahrgoh*

look at, to mirar *meerahr*
lose, to perder *pehrdhayr*
lounge sala *sahlah*
lunch comida *kohmeedhah*

mackerel caballa
kahbhahlyah
macrobiotic macrobiótico
mahkrohbeeohteekoh
Madam señora *sayniohrah*
maize maíz *maeeth*
make, to hacer *ahthehr*
management dirección
deerehkthyon
manager director
deerayktohr
manner modo *mohdhoh*
many mucho *moochoh*
March marzo *mahrthoh*
marinade escabechada
ayskahbhaychahdah
market mercado
mehrkahdhoh
marmalade mermelada
mayrmaylahdah
marrow calabaza
kahlahbhathah
match cerilla *thehreelyah*
mature estacionado
aystahthyonahdhoh;
maduro *mahdooroh*
May mayo *mahyoh*

mayonnaise mayonesa
  mighohnaysah

meal comida *kohmeedhah*

mean, to/ significar
  seegneefeekahr

mean, what does it? ¿qué
  significa? *kay
  seegneefeekah*

meat carne *kahrnay*

meatballs albóndigas
  ahlbhohndeekhahs

medicine medicina
  maydheethynah

meet, to encontrar
  aynkohntrahr

melon melón *maylon*

mention it, don't de nada
  day nahdhah

menu menú *maynoo*

message comunicación
  kohmooneekahthyon

mild dulce *doolthay*

milk leche *laychay*

mince, to triturar
  treetoorahr

minced triturado
  treetoorahdhoh

minced meat carne triturada
  kahrnay treetoorahdhah

mineral water agua mineral
  ahgwah meenayrahl

mint menta *mayntah*

minus menos *maynohs*

minute minuto *meenootoh*

Miss señorita *sayniohreetah*

mistake equivocación
  aykeevohkahthyon

misunderstanding
  malentendido
  mahlayntayndeedhoh

mixed mixto *meextoh*

mixture mezcla *maythklah*

Monday lunes *loonays*

month mes *mays*

monuments monumentos
  mohnoomayntohs

more más *mahs*

morning mañana
  mahniahnah

mosquito mosquitos
  mohskeetohs

mother madre *mahdray*

mount, to subir *soobheer*

mouth boca *bohkah*

Mrs. señora *sayniohrah*

much mucho *moochoh*

much, not poco *pohkoh*

mullet róbalo *rohbahloh*

mullet, red salmonetes
  sahlmohnaytays

museum museo *moosayoh*

mushrooms/fresh/dried
  setas/frescas/secas
  saytahs/frehskahs/saykahs

music música _moo_seekah

mussels mejillones
mehkhee_lyoh_nays

must deber day_bhayr_

mustard mostaza
mohs_tah_thah

mutton carnero kahr_nay_roh

name nombre _nohm_bray

napkin servilleta
sehrbee_lyay_tah

narrow estrecho
ay_stray_choh

nearly casi _kah_see

need necesidad
naythaysee_dhahdh_

need of, to have necesitar
naythaysee_tahr_

neighborhood alrededores
ahlraydhay_dhoh_rays

never nunca _noon_kah

New Year's Eve Nochevieja
Nohchay_byay_khah

newspaper periódico
pay_ryo_dheekoh

no no/ninguno/a
noh/neen_goo_noh/ah

nobody nadie _nah_dyay

noise ruido _rwee_dhoh

noisy ruidoso rwee_dhoh_soh

non-alcoholic, alcohol-free
sin alcohol _seen ahlkoh_ohl

none ninguno/a
neen_goo_noh/ah

non-smoker no fumador
noh foomah_dhohr_

noodles fideos finos
_fee_dhayohs _fee_nohs

no-one nadie _nah_dyay

north norte _nor_tay

nothing nada _nah_dhah

November noviembre
noh_vyaym_bray

number número
_noo_mayroh

nutcracker cascanueces
kaskah_nway_thays

nutmeg nuez moscada
noo_ayth_ moskahdah

nutrition alimentación
ahleemayntah_thyon_

oat avena ah_bay_nah

obligatory obligatorio
ohbhleegah_toh_ryoh

obtain, to obtener
obteh_nayr_

October octubre ok_too_bray

octopus pulpo _pool_poh

offal asaduras
ahsah_doo_rahs

often a menudo _ah
may_nood_hoh

oil aceite a_thay_tay

oil cruet aceitera
  athaytayrah
oil, in en aceite *ayn
  athaytay*
oily untado/grasiento
  oontahdhoh/grahsyayntoh
old viejo *byaykhoh*
olive aceitunas
  ahthaytoonahs
omelette tortilla *torteelyah*
on (prep.) encima
  aynthymah
on encendido
  aynthayndeedhoh
onion cebolla *thaybohlyah*
only solamente
  sohlahmayntay; sólo
  sohloh
open abierto *ahbhyehrtoh*
operate, to funcionar
  foonthyonahr
orange naranja
  nahrahnkhah
orangeade naranjada
  nahrahnkhahdhah
order peticion *payteethyon*
order, to ordenar/pedir
  ohrdaynahr/ pehdheer
oregano orégano
  ohraygahnoh
original auténtico
  owtaynteekoh

other otro *ohtroh*
out of order
  estropeado/destrozo
  *aystrohpayahdhoh/
  daystrohthoh*
outside externo *extayrnoh*;
  al aire libre *ahl ighray
  leebray*; fuera *fwayrah*
oven horno *ohrnoh*
overseas extranjero
  extrahnkhayroh
own propio *prohpyoh*
ox buey *bway*
oysters ostras *ohstrahs*

pacifier chupete
  choopaytay
packaged confeccionado
  kohnfaykthyonahdhoh
pain mal/dolor *mahl/
  dohlor*
pair par *pahr*
pancake oreja de abad
  oraykha day ahbahd
paper papel *pahpehl*
paper tissue pañuelo de
  papel *pahniwaylohs day
  pahpehl*
papers (passport, etc.)
  documentos
  dohkoomayntohs
parents padres *pahdrays*
park parque *pahrkay*

parking lot aparcamiento
  ahpahrkahmyayntoh
parsley perejil *payraykheel*
part parte *pahrtay*
party fiesta *fyaystah*
party (of people) pandilla
  pahndeelyah
passport pasaporte
  pahsahportay
pasta pasta *pahstah*
pastry shop pastelería
  pahstaylayreeah
pastry, short pastaflora
  pahstahflohrah
pay pagar *pahgahr*
payment pago *pahkhoh*
peach melocotón
  maylohkohton
peanut cacahuete
  kahkahwaytay
pear pera *pehrah*
peas guisantes
  gweesahntays
peel, to pelar *paylahr*
pen bolígrafo *bohleegrafoh*
pencil lápiz *lahpeeth*
pepper pimienta
  peemyayntah
pepper mill triturador de
  pimienta *treetoorahdhohr
  day peemyayntah*
per por/para *por/pahrah*

perch perca *pehrkah*
performance espectáculo
  ayspehktahkooloh
perhaps quizás *keethahs*
permission permitido
  pehrmeeteedhoh
permit permitido
  pehrmeeteedhoh
persimmon caqui *kahkee*
petit four pasta (dulce)
  pahstah (doolthay)
pharmacy farmacia
  farmahthyah
pheasant faisán *faheesahn*
phone call llamada
  telefónica *lyahmahdhah
  taylayfohneekah*
photograph fotografía
  fohtohgrahfeeah
pickled en vinagre *ayn
  beenahgray*
pie pastel *pahstayl*; tarta
  tahrtah
pig suino *sweenoh*; cerdo
  thehrdoh
pigeon pichón *peechohn*
pike lucio *loothyoh*
pill pastilla *pahsteelyah*;
  píldora *peeldohrah*
pillow almohada/
  almohadilla *ahlmohahdhah/
  ahlmohahdheelyah*

pine nuts piñones
peeniohnays
pineapple piña *peeniah*
pistachio nuts pistachos
peestahchohs
place lugar *loogahr*; sitio
seetyoh; local *lohkahl*
place, to meter/poner
maytayr/pohnayr
plain (without sauce, etc.)
sin salsa *seen sahlsah*
plate plato *plahtoh*
play, to jugar *khoogahr*
please por favor *por fahvor*
please, to placer *plahthehr*
pluck, to pelar *paylahr*
plums ciruelas
theerwaylahs
poisoning intoxicación
eentoxykahthyon
popsicle polo *pohloh*
pork suido *sweedoh*;
cerdo *thehrdoh*
portion porción *porthyon*
possible posible
pohseebhlay
postcard postal *pohstahl*
potatoes/boiled/roast
patatas/cocidas/asadas
*pahtahtahs/kohthydhahs/
asahdhahs*
power supply corriente
korryayntay

prefer, to preferir
prayfehreer
pregnant embarazada
ehmbahrathahdhah
prepare, to preparar
praypahrahr
preserved conservado
kohnsayrbahdoh
presevatives conservantes
kohnsayrbahntays
price precio *praythyoh*
pulp pulpa *poolpah*
pumpkin calabaza
kahlahbhathah
purée puré *pooray*
put out, to apagar
ahpahkhahr
put, to meter/poner
maytayr/pohnayr
quail codorniz
kohdohrneeth
quarter cuarto *kwahrtoh*
question pregunta/petición
praygoontah/payteethyohn
quick rápido *rahpeedhoh*
quickly rápidamente
rahpeedhahmayntay

rabbit conejo *kohnaykhoh*
radio radio *rahdhyoh*
radishes rábanos
rahbhahnohs

raincoat impermeable
  eempehrmayahblay

raisins uvas pasas *oovahs
  pahsahs*

raspberries fresones
  fraysohnays

raw vegetables crudeza
  kroodhethah

raw crudo *kroodhoh*

read, to leer *lehayr*

ready-made confeccionado
  kohnfaykthyonahdhoh

really propio *prohpyoh*

receipt recibo *raytheebhoh*

recipe receta *raythaytah*

red rojo *rohkhoh*

redcurrant grosella
  grohsaylyah

refrigerator frigorífico
  freegohreefeekoh

refund reembolso
  rayehmbohlsoh

region región *raykhyohn*

remain, to quedarse
  kaydahr/say

remove, to quitar *keetahr*

rent, to alquilar *ahlkeelahr*

reply, to responder
  rayspohndayr

reserve, to reservar
  rehsayrbahr

reserved reservado
  rehsehrbahdhoh

restaurant restaurante
  raystowrahntay

return regreso *raygraysoh*

return, to volver *vohlbayr*

ribs costillas *kohsteelyahs*

rice arroz *ahrroth*

right/on the right derecha/a
  la derecha *dayraychah/ah
  lah dayraychah*

ripe estacionado
  aystahthyonahdhoh;
  maduro *mahdooroh*

road calle/carreterra
  kahlyay/kahrraytayrah

roast asado *ahsahdhoh*

roasted asado *ahsahdhoh*

roll (filled) bocadillo
  bohkahdheelyoh

room (hotel) habitación
  ahbheetahthyon

room sala *sahlah*

rosemary romero
  rohmayroh

rural rústico *roosteekoh*

safety pin broche de
  seguridad *brohchay day
  saykhooreedhadh*

saffron azafrán *ahtahfrahn*

sage salvia *sahlbyah*

salad ensalada
aynsahlahdhah
salmon, smoked salmón
ahumado *sahlmon
ahoomahdhoh*
salt sal *sahl*
salt shaker salero *sahlayroh*
salted salado *sahlahdhoh*
salty salado *sahlahdhoh*
same mismo *meesmoh*
sardine sardinas
sahrdeenahs
Saturday sábado
sahbhadhoh
sauce salsa *sahlsah*
saucepan cazuela
kahthwaylah
saucepan sartén *sahrtayn*
sausage salchicha
sahlcheechah
sausages embutidos
aymbooteedhohs
savory salado *sahlahdhoh*
say, to decir *daytheer*
schedule horario *ohrahryoh*
sea mar *mahr*
seafood mariscos
mahreeskohs
season estación/ temporada
*aystahthyon
/taympohrahdhah*
season, to saborear
sahbhohrayahr

seasoning sazón *sahthon*
second segundo
saykhoondoh
sedative calmante
kahlmahntayh
see, to ver *behr*
self mismo *meesmoh*
sell, to vender *bayndayr*
September septiembre
sehptyaymbray
service servicio
sehrbeethyoh
service charge servicio
sehrbeethyoh
serviette servilleta
sehrbeelyaytah
set the table, to poner la
mesa *pohnayr lah maysah*
shake, (milk) batido
bahteedhoh
sharp ácido *ahtheedhoh*
shell cáscara *kahskahrah*
shell concha *konthyah*
shellfish crustáceos
kroostahthayohs
shellfish moluscos
mohlooskohs
shirt camisa *kahmeesah*
shop tienda *tyayndah*
shopping, to go ir de
compras *eer day
kohmprahs*

short pastry pasta flora _pahstah flohrah_
shoulder hombro _ohmbroh_
show espectáculo _ayspehktahkooloh_
show, to mostrar _mohstrahr_
shrimps gambas _gahmbahs_
shut cerrado _thehrrahdhoh_
sick enfermo _aynfehrmoh_
side dish contorno _kohntohrnoh_
side dish guarnición _gwahrneethyon_
sight vista _beestah_
signature firma _feermah_
simple simple _seemplay_
site sitio _seetyoh_
skewer, wooden palillo _pahleelyoh_
skewers broquetas _brohkaytahs_
slice rebanada/ loncha _raybhahnahdhah/lohnchah_
sliced cortado en rebanadas _kohrtahdhoh ayn raybhahnahdhahs_
sliced cold cuts embutidos _aymbooteedhohs_
slowly despacio _dayspahthyoh_
small pequeño _paykaynioh_
smell olor _ohlohr_

smoked ahumado _ahoomahdhoh_
smoker fumador _foomahdhohr_
smooth liso _leesoh_
snack merienda _mayryayndah_
snack tapa _tahpah_
snails caracoles _kahrahkohlays_
soap jabón _khahbhon_
sole lenguado _layngwahdhoh_
some algún _ahlgoon_
some algunos _ahlgoonohs_
someone alguien _ahlgyayn_; algún/o _ahlgoon/oh_
something algo _ahlgoh_
son hijo _eekhoh_
song canción _kahnthyon_
sorbet, sherbet sorbete _sohrbaytay_
sort género _khaynayroh_
soup caldo _kahldhoh_
soup sopa _sohpah_
sour áspero _ahspayroh_; agrio _ahgryoh_
south sur _soor_
soya soja _sohkhah_
sparkling espumoso/con mucho gas _ayspoomohsoh/kon moochoh gas_

sparkling mineral water
agua con gas _ahgwah kon gas_

spices especias _ayspaythyahs_

spicy picante _peekahntay_

spinach espinacas _ayspeenahkahs_

spirits, (high-proof)
superalcohólicos _superalcolicos_

spit asador _ahsahdhohr_

spoon/teaspoon
cuchara/cucharilla _koochahrah/koochahree koochareelyah_

spring lamb cordero _kohrdayroh_

square plaza _plahthah_

squid calamares _kahlahmahrays_

stairs escaleras _ayskahlayrahs_

stamp sello _saylyoh_

start inicio _eeneethyoh_

station estación _aystahthyon_

stay, to quedarse _kaydahr/say_

steak bistec _beestayk_

steak, grilled bistec a la plancha _beestayk ah lah plahnchah_

steamed al vapor _ahl bapor_

stew carne a trozos/estofada _kahrnay ah trohthohs /aystohfahdhah_

stew estofado _aystohfahdhoh_

still todavía _tohdhahveeah_

stomachache dolor de estómago _dohlor day aystohmahgoh_

stop (bus, train, etc.)
parada _pahrahdhah_

stop, to parar _pahrahr_

stop, to (cease) dejar _dehkhahr_

stout c. oscura _c. ohskoorah_

straight (drink) liso _leesoh_

straight away enseguida _aynsaygweedah_

straight on derecho _dayraychoh_

strawberry fresa _fraysah_

street calle/carreterra _kahlyay/kahrraytayrah_

strong fuerte _fwehrtay_

stuffed relleno _raylyaynoh_

stuffed relleno _raylyaynoh_

subtle sutil _sooteel_

subway metro _mehtroh_

sugar azúcar _ahthookahr_

sugar bowl azucarero
ahthookararyroh

suitcase maleta _mahlaytah_

summer verano _bayrahnoh_

summer (adj.) veraniego /
de verano
_behrahnyaygoh/day
bayrahnoh_

Sunday domingo
dohmeengoh

surname apellido
ahpaylyeedhoh

surroundings alrededores
ahlraydhaydhohrays

sweet caramelo
kahrahmayloh

sweet dulce _doolthay_

sweet-and-sour agridulce
ahkhreedoolthay

sweetener dulcificante
doolthyfeekahntay

sweets dulces _doolthays_

swim, to nadar _nahdhahr_

swimming pool piscina
peestheenah

Switzerland Suiza
Sweethah

swordfish pez espada
pehth ayspahdhah

syrup (in) (de) jarabe _(day)_
kharahbhay

table mesa _maysah_

tablecloth mantel _mahntayl_

take, to coger/tomar
kohkhehr/tohmahr

talcum powder polvos de
talco _poalbohs day
tahlkoh_

tangerine mandarina
mahndahreenah

tart pastel _pahstayl_

tart tarta _tahrtah_

tart agrio _ahkhryoh_

tart torta, pastel glaseado
_tortah, pahstehl
glaysayahdhoh_

taste degustación
daygoostahthyon

taste gusto _goostoh_

taste sabor _sahbhohr_

taste, to degustar
daygoostahr

taste, to probar/ catar
provahr /kahtahr

tasting degustación
daygoostahthyon

tavern bodega _bodhaygah_

tavern tasca _tahskah_

tea té _tay_

tea cake pasta (dulce)
pahstah (doolthay)

telephone teléfono
taylayfohnoh

telephone directory guía
telefónica _gweeah
taylayfohneekah_

temperature temperatura
taympayrahtoorah

temperature, room
temperatura del tiempo
_taympayrahtoorah dayl
tyaympoh_

tender blando _blahndhoh_

terminus terminal de parada
_tehrmeenahl day
pahrahdhah_

terrace terraza _tayrathah_

thank you gracias
grahthyahs

thank, to agradecer
ahgrahdhaythayr

that ese/aquel _aysah/ahkayl_

that que _kay_

then después _dayspways_

thin delgado/sin grasa
daylhahdhoh/seen grahsah

thin sutil _sooteel_

thirst sed _saydh_

this este _aystay_

thousand mil _meel_

thread hilo _eeloh_

throat garganta
gahrgahntah

throw away, to tirar _teerahr_

Thursday jueves
khwayvays

thyme tomillo _tohmeelyoh_

ticket billete _beelyaytay_

tie corbata _korbahtah_

tight estrecho _aystraychoh_

time tiempo _tyaympoh_

timetable horario _ohrahryoh_

tin lata _lahtah_

tip propina _prohpeenah_

to have tener _taynayr_

toast (with glasses) brindis
breendees

toasted tostado
tohstahdhoh

toasted tostado
tohstahdhoh

tobacconist's estanco
ehstahnkoh

today hoy _oy_

together juntos/as
khoontohs/ahs

toilet baño _bahnioh_

toilet, restroom baño
bahnioh

tomato tomate _tohmahtay_

tomorrow mañana
mahniahnah

tongue lengua _layngwah_

too demasiado
daymahsyahdhoh

too much demasiado
daymahsyahdhoh

toothpick palillo
pahleelyoh

tour vuelta _bwehltah_
toward(s) hacia _ahthyah_
towel toalla _tohahlyah_
train tren _trayn_
transport/means of t.
transporte, medios de
transporte
trahnspohrtay/maydhyohs
day t.
tray bandeja _bandaykhah_
trip excursión _exkoorsyon_
tripe callos _kahlyohs_
trout trucha _troochah_
truffle trufa _troofah_
try, to probar _provahr_
Tuesday martes _mahrtays_
tuna atún _ahtoon_
turbot rombo _rohmboh_
tureen tarrina _tahrreenah_
turkey pavo _pahvoh_
turn vuelta _bwehltah_
turn off, to apagar
ahpahkhahr
turn on, to encender
aynthayndhayr
turn, to dar vueltas _dahr_
bwehltahs
type género _khaynayroh_

ugly feo _fehoh_
umbrella paraguas

uncap, to destapar
daystahpahr
uncomfortable incómodo
eenkohmohdhoh
uncork, to destapar
daystahpahr
under debajo _daybhahkhoh_
underground (train) metro
mehtroh
understand, to entender
ayntayndhayr
United States Estados
Unidos _Aystahdhohs_
Ooneedhohs
until hasta _ahstah_
use, to usar _oosahr_

vacant libre _leebray_
vacation vacaciones
bahkahthyohnays
vacation vacaciones
bhahkahtheebhnays
vanilla vainilla _bighneelyah_
veal ternero/a
tehrnayroh/ah
vegetables hortalizas
ohrtahlythahs
vegetables verdura
bayrdoorah
vegetables legumbres
laygoombrays
vegetarian vegetariano

vending machine
distribuidor
deestreebweedohr

very muy *mwee*

village pueblo *pwaybloh*

vinegar vinagre *beenahgray*

vintage (year) temporada
taympohrahdhah

vitamins vitaminas
beetahmeenahs

wait, to esperar *ayspayrahr*

waiter/waitress camarero/a
kahmahrayroh/ah

walk, to caminar
kahmeenahr

wall pared/ muro
pahrayd/mooroh

wallet cartera *kahrtayrah*

walnuts nueces *nwaythays*

want, to querer *kayrayr*

warm, to calentar
kahlayntahr

warn, to advertir
ahdbehrteer

wash, to lavar *labhar*

wasp avispa *ahbeespah*

watch reloj *rehlokh*

watermelon sandía
sahndeeah

water agua *ahgwah*

waterproof impermeable

way modo *mohdhoh*

weak débil *daybheel*

Wednesday miércoles
myayrkohlays

week semana s*aymahnah*

weekday diario *deeahreeoh*

welcome bienvenido /a
beeaynbayneedhoh/ah

welcome, you're de nada
day nahdhah

well bien *byayn*

what cual *kwahl*

what? ¿qué? *kay*

whatever cualquier/ a
kwahlkyehr/ah

when cuando *kwahndoh*

where donde *dohnday*

whereas mientras
meeayntrahs

which cual *kwahl*

which one cual *kwahl*

while mientras
meeayntrahs

whip up, to batir *bahteer*

white blanco *blahnkoh*

whiting pescadilla
peskahdheelyah

who quien *kyuyh*

whole entero *ayntayroh*

wholemeal integral

why porque *porkay*
wife mujer *mookhehr*
wild berries frutos selváticos *frootohs saylbahteekohs*
window ventana *behntahnah*
wine vino *beenoh*; **full-bodied w.** v. fuerte, v. de cuerpo *b. fwehrtay, b. kwehrpoh*; **light w.** v. ligero *b. leekhayroh*; **old (good quality) w.** v. de solera *b. day sohlayrah*; **red w.** v. tinto *b. teentoh*; **rosé w.** v. rosé/rosado *b. rosay/rohsahdhoh*; **white w.** v. blanco *b. blahnkoh*
wine cellar bodega *bodhaygah*
wineshop bodega *bodhaygah*
winter invierno *eenbyayrnoh*
wire hilo *eeloh*
with con *kon*

without sin *seen*
woman mujer *mookhehr*
word palabra *pahlahbrah*
work trabajo *trahbhahkhoh*
work, to (machine, etc.) funcionar *foonthyonahr*
wrapped-up confeccionado *kohnfaykthyonahdhoh*
write, to escribir *ayskreebheer*

year año *ahnioh*
yeast levadura *laybahdoorah*
yellow amarillo *ahmahreelyoh*
yesterday ayer *ighehr*
yet todavía *tohdhahveeah*
yolk yema *yaymah*
young joven *khohvehn*
young woman señorita *sayniohreetah*

zucchini calabacines *kahlahbhatheenays*

abajá de Algeciras see "Regional Dishes" page 37

abajo down

abierto open

abrebotellas bottle opener

abrelatas can opener

abrigo overcoat

abril April

aceite oil

aceitera oil cruet

aceitunas olives

acelgas chard

aceptar con agrado to appreciate; to accept with pleasure

achicoria chicory

ácido acid

adelante forward

aditivo additive

adulto adult

advertir to point out; to notify; to inform; to warn

aeropuerto airport

afuega'l pitu see "Cheeses", page 8

agosto August

agradecer to thank

agridulce sweet-and-sour

agridulce, al see "Gastronomic Terms", page 53

agrio sour; bitter

agua water; **aguardiente** brandy; **agua con gas** sparkling mineral water; **agua mineral** mineral water

ahumado smoked

aire air; **aire acondicionado** air-conditioning

aire libre, al outside

ajo garlic

albahaca basil

albaricoque apricot

Albariño see "Wines", page 23

albóndigas meatballs, see "The Basics", page 27

alcachofa artichoke

alcachofas rellenas stuffed artichokes , see "National Dishes", page 28

alcaparras capers

alcohólico alcoholic

alcublas see "Wines", page 23

alemán German

Alemania Germany

alergia allergy

algo something; anything

algodón cotton

alguien someone; somebody; anybody

algún some; someone

algunos some; a few (pl)

Alicante see "Cheeses", page 8

ali-oli see "Gastronomic Terms", page 53

almidón starch

alimentación nutrition; diet

almeja clam, see "Seafood", page 17; **almejas a la marinera** clam marinara, see "National Dishes", page 28 and "Recipes", page 57; **almejas guisadas** see "National Dishes", page 28

almendras almonds

almendras garrapiñadas see "Sweets, Cakes, and Pastries", page 20

al menos at least

almíbar en see "Gastronomic Terms", page 55

almohada / almohadilla cushion; pillow

alquiler rent; hire

alrededores neighborhood; surroundings

alubias beans

amargo bitter

amarillo yellow

a menudo often

amigo friend

anchoa anchovy

andoya see "Cold Cut Meats", page 13

anguila eel; **anguilas al horno** baked eel, see "National Dishes", page 28; **anguilas con guisantes** eel and peas, see "National Dishes", page 28

angulas a la cazuela, see "Regional Dishes", page 39; **angulas a la vasca** Basque-style eel fries, see "Regional Dishes", page 48

ángulo angle

anís anise; aniseed

antes before

antibiótico antibiotic

año year

apagar to turn off; to put out

aparcamiento car park; parking lot

apellido surname

aperitivo aperitif

apetito appetite

apio celery

aquí here

arenque herring

Armada see "Cheeses", page 8

aroma aroma; fragrance

aromático aromatic

arroz rice; **arroz a la zamorana** see "Regional Dishes", page 42; **arroz amb fesols y naps**, see "Regional Dishes", page 51; **arroz blanco** white rice, see "National Dishes", page 28; **arroz con almejas** rice and clams, see "National Dishes", page 29; **arroz con costra** see "Regional Dishes", page 51; **arroz con leche** see "Sweets, Cakes, and Pastries", page 20; **arroz con riñones** rice and kidneys, see "National Dishes", page 29

asado roast

asador spit

asaduras entrails; offal; giblets

ascensor lift

áspero sour; bitter

aspirina aspirin

atento attentive; alert

atún tuna; **atún asado** baked tuna, see "National Dishes", page 29; **atún con tomate** tuna and tomato, see "National Dishes", page 29

Austria Austria

austríaco Austrian

auténtico authentic; genuine; original

autobús bus

avellanas hazelnuts

avión airplane

ayer yesterday

ayudar to help

azafrán saffron

azúcar sugar

azucarero sugar bowl

bacalao dried salted cod; **bacalao al pil pil**, see "Regional Dishes", page 48; **bacalao a la vizcaína** see "Regional Dishes", page 48; **bacalao al horno** baked dried salted cod, see "National Dishes", page 29

bailar to dance

banco bank

bandeja tray

baño toilet, bathroom

bar bar; café

barato economical; cheap; inexpensive

Barcelona Barcelona

bastar to be sufficient; to be enough

batido (milk) shake

batir to beat; to whip up; to whisk

beber to drink

bebida drink

bechamel see "The Basics", page 27

berberecho see "Seafood", page 17

berenjena eggplant

berza cabbage

besugo sea bream; **besugo al horno** baked sea bream, see "National Dishes", page 29; **besugo a la madrileña** Madrid-style sea bream. see "Regional Dishes", page 43

Betanzos see "Wines", page 23

Beyos, queso de los see "Cheeses", page 11

bien well; good

bienvenido welcome

Bierzo see "Wines", page 23

bígaro see "Seafood", page 17

billete ticket

biscotes biscuits

bistec a la plancha grilled steak

bizcochos see "Sweets, Cakes, and Pastries", page 20

blanco white

blando tender

blancos see "Cold Cut Meats", page 13

blanquet see "Cold Cut Meats", page 13

boca mouth

bocadillo (filled) roll, see "Gastronomic Terms", page 54

bodega (wine) cellar

bolígrafo pen

Boloña Bologna

bolso bag

bonito beautiful; handsome

botella bottle

botelo see "Cold Cut Meats", page 13

borlas flakes

botón button

bovino bovine, beef

brasa coals; cinders; embers

brazo arm; **brazo de gitano** see "Sweets, Cakes, and Pastries", page 20

brindis toast

bueno good

buey ox; beef **buey de mar** see "Seafood", page 17

buñuelos fritters, see "Sweets, Cakes, and Pastries", page 20;

buñuelos de manzanas see "Regional Dishes" page 51;

Burgos see "Cheeses", page 8

burrida de ratjada see "Regional Dishes", page 40

butifarra see "Cold Cut Meats", page 14

caballa mackerel

cabra goat

cabrales see "Cheeses", page 9

cabrito asado see "National Dishes", page 29

cacahuete peanut

cacao cocoa

cachuela extremeña see "Regional Dishes" page 43

cada each; every

caerse to fall

café coffee; **café cortado** white coffee; **café con leche** cappuccino; **café descafeinado** decaffeinated; **café solo** black coffee

caja cash desk; checkout

cajera cashier

calabacines zucchini

calabaza pumpkin; gourd; marrow

calamares squid; **calamares a la romana** see "National Dishes", page 29; **calamares en su tinta** squid, see "National Dishes", page 30

caldeirada de pescado see "Regional Dishes" page 46

caldereta asturiana see "Regional Dishes" page 39; **caldereta de Cordero** see "Regional Dishes" page 42; **caldereta de langosta** see "Regional Dishes" page 40; **caldereta extremeña** see "Regional Dishes" page 43

caldo broth; soup; **caldo gallego** Galician broth, see "Regional Dishes" page 46, and "Recipes", page 58

calefacción heating

calentar to heat; to warm

caliente hot

calle street; road

callos tripe, see "National Dishes", page 30 and "Recipes", page 59; **callos a la madrileña** see "Regional Dishes" page 44

calmante sedative

calorías calories

camarero/a waiter/waitress

cambiar to change

cambio exchange rate

caminar to walk

camisa shirt

camomila camomile

campesina, a la see "Gastronomic Terms", page 53

campo field; countryside

canapés see "Other Specialties", page 25

canción song

canelones cannelloni, see "National Dishes", page 30

cangrejo crab; **cangrejo de mar** see "Seafood", page 17; **cangrejos de río** river crabs, see "Regional Dishes" page 43

caracoles snails; **caracoles pagesos** see "Regional Dishes" page 40; **caracoles a la riojana** see "Regional Dishes" page 49

caramelo caramel; sweet; candy

cardos cardoon

cargar en cuenta to debit; to charge

carne meat; **carne a trozos** stew; **carne de cerdo con leche** see "Regional Dishes", page 40; **carne en lata** canned meat;

carne mechada see "National Dishes", page 30; **carne triturada** minced meat

carnero mutton; lamb

carnet de identidad identity card

carnicería butcher

caro expensive; dear

cartera wallet

casa house; **de la casa** see "Gastronomic Terms", page 54

cáscara door

casero homemade

casi almost

castaña chestnut

catar to taste; to try

Cava see "Wines", page 23

caviar caviar

caza game; hunting

cazuela (cooking) pot; saucepan; **a la cazuela** see "Gastronomic Terms", page 53

cebolla onion

cedro citron

cecina see "Cold Cut Meats", page 14

cena dinner

cenicero ashtray

ceniza ash

centollo see "Seafood", page 18

central central

centro centre

cepillo brush

cerdo pig; pork

cerebro brain

cerebro see "Cheeses", page 9

cerezas cherries

cerilla match

cerrado closed

cerrar to close

cerveza beer; **c. clara** lager; **c. de barril** draught; **c. grande** large; **c. oscura** stout; **c. pequeña** small

ciento hundred

cierre closure

cigala see "Seafood", page 18

cigarrillo cigarette

cigarro cigar

ciruelas plum

cita appointment; date

ciudad city

clara de huevo eggwhite

claro clear; pale

cliente client; customer

coca see "Regional Dishes" page 40

cocer to cook

cocido boiled; cooked **cocido madrileño** see "National Dishes", page 30; "Recipes", page 60; "Regional Dishes", page 44

cocinero cook

cocción cooking; baking

coco coconut

coche automobile; car

cochecito de niños pram; baby carriage

cochifrito see "Regional Dishes" page 49

cochinillo piglet **cochinillo asado** roast piglet, see "Regional Dishes", page 43; see "National Dishes", page 30

codorniz quail; **codorniz en su salsa** see "National Dishes", page 31

coger to take

coliflor cauliflower; **coliflor frita** fried cauliflower, see "National Dishes", page 31

color color

colorantes coloring agents

comenzar to start; to begin

comer to eat

comida lunch

como how; like; as; such as

cómodo convenient; comfortable

compota de manzana see "National Dishes", page 31

compra expense; **ir de compras** to go shopping

comprar to buy

comprendido included; inclusive

comunicación communication; announcement; message

con with

concha shell

conejo rabbit, see "National Dishes", page 31; **conejo con peras** rabbit and pears, see "Regional Dishes" page 45

con gas fizzy

congrio conger; **congrio con almejas** conger eel and clam, see "National Dishes", page 31

con hielo with ice

con mantequilla buttered; with butter

confeccionado packaged; wrapped-up; ready-made

confeti sugar-coated almonds

confirmar to confirm

congelado frozen

conservantes preservatives

contado, al in cash

contento happy; content

continuar to continue

contra against

controlar to control; to check

copa dish; tub

corbata tie

cordero spring lamb; **cordero en chilindrón** see "Regional Dishes" page 48

corposo full-bodied; thick; dense

corriente power supply; current

cortado cut; chopped

cortar to cut

cosa thing

costar to cost

coste cost

costilla cutlet; chop

crema catalana see "Sweets, Cakes, and Pastries", page 20

crianza breeding; farming (of animals)

cristal glass; crystal

croissant croissant

croqueta croquette

crudeza raw vegetables

crudo raw; uncooked
crujiente crisp; crunchy
crustáceos shellfish
cual what; which; which one
cualquiera any; whatever
cuando when
cuanto how much; how many
cuarto fourth; quarter
cubiertos cutlery
cubito ice-cube
cubrir to cover
cuchara spoon
cucharilla teaspoon
cuchillo knife
cuenta bill; account
cuidar to keep; to guard
cuinat see "Regional Dishes" page 41

champán champagne
chanfaina see "National Dishes", page 31 and "Regional Dishes", page 37
chaqueta jacket
cheque check; cheque
Cheste see "Wines", page 23
chico/a boy/girl
chipirones en su tinta see "Regional Dishes" page 48;

chipirones fritos see "National Dishes", page 31; **chipirones rellenos** see "Regional Dishes" page 48
chirlas small clams, see "Seafood", page 18
chistorra see "Cold Cut Meats", page 14
chocolate chocolate
chorizo red salami, see "Cold Cut Meats", page 14
chuleta chop; **chuletas/chuletillas de cordero** spring-lamb cutlets, see "National Dishes", page 31; **chuletas a la aragonesa** see "Regional Dishes" page 50
chuletón giant steak, see "National Dishes", page 31
Chulilla see "Wines", page 23
chupete dummy; pacifier
churrasco grilled meat
churros see "Sweets, Cakes, and Pastries", page 20

dar to give
dar vueltas to turn
dátiles dates
debajo under
deber to have to; must

débil weak
decir to say
decoración decoration
decorado decorated
degustación taste; tasting
degustar to taste; to enjoy
dejar to leave; to stop
delgado thin; lean
demasiado too much; too
de nada don't mention it!;
  you're welcome!
dentadura postiza dentures;
  set of false teeth
dentón dentex (fish)
dentro (de) in; inside
depositar to deposit
derecha right
desinfectante disinfectant
desinfectar to disinfect
después after; then
destapar to uncork
desvanecido fainted
detrás behind
día day
diabético diabetic
diario weekday
diciembre December
dieta diet
difícil difficult
diga Hello? (telephone)
digerible digestible

digestivo digestive
dinero silver
dinero suelto (small) change
dirección address
director manager; director
discoteca discothéque;
  disco
distancia distance
distinto different
distribuidor distributor;
  vending machine
divisa currency
doble double
documento document
dólares dollars
dolor pain
dolor de barriga bellyache;
  dolor de estómago
  stomachache; **dolor de
  cabeza** headache
domingo Sunday
donde where
dorada gilthead bream;
  dorada a la sal see
  "Regional Dishes", page 51
dorado browned; golden
  brown
dulce sweet; mild
dulces sweets; candies;
  confectionery
dulcificante sweetener
duro hard

embajada embassy

embarazada pregnant

embutidos sausages; cold cut meats; **embutidos mixtos** see "National Dishes", page 32

empanada see "Other Specialties", page 25; **empanada gallega** see "Regional Dishes" page 46

empanadas see "Regional Dishes" page 41

empanadilla see "Other Specialties", page 25

empanado breaded

emparedados canapé

en aceite in oil

en cambio instead (of)

encéfalo brain

encender to light; to turn on

encendido lit; on

encima on; above

endivia endive

enfermar to fall ill; to be taken ill

enfermo ill; sick

enfriar to cool

ensaimadas see "Sweets, Cakes, and Pastries", page 21; see "Regional Dishes" page 41

ensalada salad

ensaladilla rusa Russian salad, see "National Dishes", page 32

en seguida at once; straight away

entender to understand

entero whole

entrada entry; entrance

entrar to enter

entre amongst; within; between

entrecote de ternera see "National Dishes", page 32

entremés hors-d'oeuvres; appetizer

en vinagre pickled

equivocación mistake

error error

escabechada marinade

escabeche pickled in vinegar, see "Gastronomic Terms", page 55

escaldón canario see "Regional Dishes" page 41

escaleras stairs

escalivada see "Regional Dishes" page 45

escalopes breaded minute steaks, see "The Basics", page 27

escribir to write

escudella see "Regional Dishes" page 45

España Spain

español Spanish

espárragos asparagus, see "National Dishes", page 32

especias spices; aromatic herbs

espectáculo show; performance

esperar to hope; to wait

espinacas spinach

estación station; season

Estados Unidos United States

estanco tobacconist's

esta noche this evening

este this

estofado stew; **estofado a la asturiana** see "Regional Dishes", page 39; **estofado de buey** beef stew, see "Regional Dishes", page 39

estrecho narrow; tight

estropeado broken; out of order; (mechanical) failure

estudiar to study

evitar to avoid

excepto except

excursión excursion; trip

experto expert

exposición exhibition

externo external; outside

extranjero foreign; foreigner; overseas

fabada asturiana see "Regional Dishes" page 39 and "Recipes", page 61

fabes con almejes see "Regional Dishes" page 39

fácil easy

factura invoice

faisán pheasant

familia family

familiar familiar; family (adj)

famoso famous

farmacéutico chemist; pharmacist

fariñón see "Cold Cut Meats" page 14

farmacia chemist's; pharmacy; drugstore

favor, por please

febrero February

feo bad; ugly

fiambre mixed sausages, see "Gastronomic Terms", page 55

fideos noodles

fideua see "Regional Dishes" page 51

fiesta party; fête; public holiday

filete (de carne) minute steak, see "The Basics", page 27

filetes fillets

filetes de ternera see "National Dishes", page 32

filetes empanados breaded minute steaks, see "National Dishes", page 32

filtrar to filter

filloas see "Regional Dishes" page 46

fin end

firma signature

flan see "Sweets, Cakes, and Pastries", page 21

flaó see "Regional Dishes" page 41

flores flowers

floristería florist

fotografía photograph

francés French

Francia France

freír to fry

fresa strawberry

fresco fresh, cool

fresones raspberries

frigorífico refrigerator

frío cold

frito fried

fritura frying; fried food; fry; fry-up

frixuelos see "Regional Dishes" page 39

fruta fruit

frutos selváticos wild berries

fuego fire

fuera outside

fuet see "Cold Cut Meats", page 15

fumador smoker

funcionar to work; to function; to run; to operate

gallina hen; **gallina en pepitoria** see "Regional Dishes", page 48

gallo cock

gallo capado capon

gallo pequeño cockerel; young cock

gambas prawns, see "Seafood", page 18

gamonedo see "Cheeses", page 9

garbanzos chick-peas

garganta throat

garrafa carafe; jug; decanter

gazpacho andaluz see "Regional Dishes" page 30

gelatina gelatin; jelly

género kind; sort; type; gender

Génova Genoa

gorbea see "Cheeses", page 9

gordo fat

gracias thank you

Gran Bretaña Great Britain

grande big; large; great

granizado water ice

graso fat

gratén, al see "Gastronomic Terms", page 53

gratinado (au) gratin

gratinado de berenjenas aubergines au gratin see "National Dishes", page 32 and "Regional Dishes", page 44

gratis for free; for nothing; without charge

grosella blackcurrant

grupo group

guantes gloves

guarda caretaker; guardian; keeper

guardarropa cloakroom

guarnición vegetables; side dish

guía guide

guía telefónica phone book

guinda sour cherry drink; sour (black) cherry

guindilla hot pepper; chili pepper

guisado de trigo see "Regional Dishes", page 51

guisantes peas

guiso gravy

guiso de caracoles see "Regional Dishes" page 38

guiso de rabo de toro see "Regional Dishes", page 38

gusto taste; flavor

habas broad beans

habitación room

hacer to do; to make

hambre hunger

harina flour

Haro see "Wines", page 23

hasta until; as far as

heladería ice-cream shop

helado ice-cream, see "Sweets, Cakes, and Pastries", page 21

hervir to boil

hielo ice

hierbas, a las see "Gastronomic Terms", page 53

higadillos chicken liver

hígado liver

hijo son
hilo thread; line; wire
hinojo fennel; **hinojos con jamón** fennel and ham, see "Regional Dishes", page 50
hoja leaf, sheet of paper
hojaldre cream puff
Holanda Holland
hombre man
hombro shoulder
homogeneizado homogenized; baby food
hora hour
hora, a la on time
horario timetable; schedule
horno oven; **al horno** see "Gastronomic Terms", page 53
hortalizas vegetables
hospital hospital
hotel hotel
hueso bone
huevos eggs; **h. al plato** see "National Dishes", page 32; **h. a la flamenca** see "Regional Dishes", page 38; **h. con mantequilla** eggs fried in butter; **h. duros** hard-boiled eggs; **h. revueltos** scrambled eggs

humeante smoking; steaming
humo smoke

idiazábal see "Cheeses", page 10
igual equal
impermeable waterproof; raincoat
importancia, a la see "Gastronomic Terms", page 53
importante important
imposible impossible
incluido included
incómodo uncomfortable; awkward; inconvenient
indicaciones directions; indications
información information
informar informer
Inglaterra England
inglés English
inicio start; beginning
inocuo harmless; inoffensive
insecto insect
integral total; complete; wholemeal; integral
interior internal; interior
interno internal; inside; (telephone) extension

interurbana long-distance call

intoxicación poisoning; intoxication

invierno winter

invitar to invite

ir to go

Irlanda Ireland

irse to leave; to depart

Italia Italy

italiano Italian

jabón soap

jamón ham, see "Cold Cut Meats", page 15; **jamón con guisantes** ham and peas, see "National Dishes", page 32

jarabe syrup

jardín garden

jardinera, a la see "Gastronomic Terms", page 54

jarra jug

jefe chef , chief

Jerez see "Wines", page 23; **al Jerez** see "Gastronomic Terms", page 54

joven young

judías con chorizo see "Regional Dishes", page 50

judías verdes French beans, see "National Dishes", page 33

judiones broad beans; **judiones de la granja** see "Regional Dishes", page 43

juego game

jueves Thursday

jugar to play

julio July

Jumilla see "Wines", page 24

junio June

juntar to join; to gather; to put together

junto a beside; next to

kaki persimmon

kiwi kiwi fruit

lacón see "Cold Cut Meats", page 15; **lacón con grelos** see "Regional Dishes", page 46

lago lake

langosta lobster, see "Seafood", page 18

langostino baby lobster, see "Seafood", page 18; see "National Dishes", page 33

lápiz pencil

largo long

las mijas see "Regional Dishes", page 44

lata tin; can

laurel bay leaf

lavar to wash

Lebeña, quesucos de see "Cheeses", page 11

lechazo castellano see "Regional Dishes", page 43

leche milk

lechuga lettuce

leer to read

legumbres legumes

lejos far

lengua tongue

lenguado sole; **lenguado al horno** baked sole, see "National Dishes", page 33

lenguas de gato see "Sweets, Cakes, and Pastries", page 21

lente lens

lentejas lentils; **lentejas al estilo de Burgos** see "Regional Dishes", page 44; **lentejas con sobrasada** see "Regional Dishes", page 41

lentillas contact lenses

León see "Cheeses", page 10

levadura yeast

libre free; clear; vacant

libro book

licor liqueur

liebre hare

ligero light

limón lemon

limpiar to clean

limpio clean

línea line

liso smooth; straight

lista list

listo ready

litro liter

local local; room; place; premises; bar

lomo embuchado, loin, see "Cold Cut Meats", page 15

longaniza see "Cold Cut Meats", page 15

Los Oteros see "Wines", page 24

lubina bass; **lubina asada** oven-baked sea bass, see "National Dishes", page 33

lucio pike

lugar place

lunes Monday

luz light

llama flame

llamada telefónica phone call

llamar to call; to phone
llegar to arrive
lleno full
lleno de gente crowded
llevar to bring; to carry; to wear

macedonia fruit salad
macrobiótico macrobiotic
madre mother
Madrid Madrid
maduro ripe; mature
maíz maize; corn
mal/o bad; evil
malentendido misunderstanding
maleta suitcase
mañana morning; tomorrow; tomorrow morning
mandarina tangerine
manjar dish; (main) course
mano hand
manteca lard
mantel tablecloth
mantequilla butter
manzana apple; **manzanas al horno** see "Sweets, Cakes, and Pastries", page 21; **manzanas rellenas de nuez y cocco** see "National Dishes", page 33

mar sea
marido husband
marinera, a la see "Gastronomic Terms", page 54
mariscos seafood
marrones chestnuts
martes Tuesday
marzo March
más more
masticar to chew; to masticate
mayo May
mayonesa mayonnaise
medicina medicine
médico doctor
medio half; means
mejor better; best
mejillones mussels, see "Seafood" page 18; **mejillones al vapor** steamed mussels, see "National Dishes", page 33; **mejillones al vino blanco** mussels in white wine sauce, see "Regional Dishes", page 47
melocotón peach
melón melon
menestra soup, see "National Dishes", page 33
menos less; minus

menta mint
menú menu
mercado market
merienda snack
merluza hake; **merluza a la cazuela** hake casserole, see "National Dishes", page 33 and "Recipes", page 63; **merluza a la sidra** cidered hake, see "Regional Dishes", page 40; **merluza a la vasca** see "Regional Dishes", page 49
mermelada jam
mes month
mesa table
metro subway
mezcla blend; mixture
mezclar to mix; to blend
miel honey
mientras while; whereas
miércoles Wednesday
migas see "Other Specialties", page 25
mil thousand
milhojas see "National Dishes", page 33
minusválido disabled
minuto minute
mirar to watch; to look at
mitad half

mismo same; self
mixto mix; mixed
modo way; manner
molestar to disturb
mollejas sweetbread
moluscos molluscs; shellfish
moneda coin
Monterrey see "Wines", page 24
Montilla see "Wines", page 24
Montroy see "Wines", page 24
monumentos monuments
morcilla see "National Dishes", page 33; see "Cold Cut Meats", page 15
morcón see "Cold Cut Meats", page 15
morros de ternera a la asturiana see "Regional Dishes", page 40
morteruelo see "Regional Dishes", page 44
mosca fly
mosquitos mosquito; gnat
mostaza mustard
mostrar to show
mucho a lot; much; very
mujer woman; wife
muro wall
museo museum

música music
muslo thigh
muy many, very

nada nothing
nadar to swim
nadie no; nobody; none
naranja orange; **naranjada**
orangeade
nata cream; **nata con**
nueces see "National
Dishes", page 34; **nata**
líquida single cream; **nata**
montada whipped cream
natillas flan, see "Sweets,
Cakes, and Pastries", page
21
natural, al see
"Gastronomic Terms",
page 54
Navidad Christmas
necesidad need
necesitar to have need of
nécora see "Seafood", page
19
negro black
ningún/o no one; nobody
no fumador non-smoking
noche night
Nochebuena Christmas Eve
Nochevieja New Year's Eve
nombre name

norte north
noviembre November
novillo beef
nueces walnuts
nuez moscada nutmeg
número number
nunca never

obligar to oblige; to force;
to compel
obligatorio compulsory;
obligatory
obtener to obtain
oca goose
octubre October
ocupado busy; engaged;
taken
oír to hear; to feel
ojo eye
olor smell; odor
olvidar to forget
olla gitana see "Regional
Dishes", page 38; **olla**
podrida see "Regional
Dishes", page 50
ordenar to order
orduña see "Cheeses", page
10
orégano oregano; marjoram
oro gold
oscuro dark

ostra oyster, see "Seafood", page 19

otro other

padre father

padres parents

paella see "National Dishes", page 34; **paella valenciana** see "Recipes", page 63 and see "Regional Dishes", page 52

pagar to pay

pago payment

país country; land; village; town

palabra word

palillo toothpick; wooden skewer

paloma dove

pan bread

pan de molde loaf of bread

pan rallado breadcrumbs

pandilla party; group; company

pañuelo handkerchief; **pañuelo de papel** paper tissue

papel paper

par pair

para for; per; in order to

parada stop

paraguas umbrella

parar to stop

parrilla grill; **a la parrilla** see "Gastronomic Terms", page 54

parque park

parte part

pasaporte passport

pasiego see "Cheeses", page 10

pasta pasta

pastel tart; cake; pie; **pastel de la abuela** see "Sweets, Cakes, and Pastries", page 21

pastelería cakeshop

pastillas pill; **pastiglia de avecrem** stock (bouillon) cube

patatas potatoes; **patatas a la riojana** see "Regional Dishes", page 50; **patatas asadas** roast potatoes; **patatas cocidas** boiled potatoes; **patatas con carne** meat and potatoes, see "National Dishes", page 34; **patatas fritas** chips; French fries

pato duck; **pato al horno** Roast duck, see "National Dishes", page 34

pavo turkey

pecho breast; chest

pechugas de pollo see "National Dishes", page 34
pedir to ask
pelar to pluck; to peel
pencas de acelga gratinada see "Regional Dishes", page 50
pendientes earrings
pepinos cucumbers
pequeño small
pera pear
perca perch
percebe see "Seafood", page 19
perder to lose
perdices con chocolate see "Regional Dishes", page 49
perdiz partridge; **perdiz estofada** see "Regional Dishes", page 44
perejil parsley
periódico newspaper
permitido permission; permit
permitir to permit; to allow
pescadilla whiting
pescado fish
pestiños see "Regional Dishes", page 52
petición request; demand
picadillo see "National Dishes", page 34

picante hot; spicy
pichón pigeon
picón de Tresviso see "Cheeses", page 10
pie foot
pierna leg
píldora pill
pimentón hot and mild red bell pepper powder
pimienta pepper
pimiento bell pepper; **pimientos rellenos** stuffed bell peppers, see "National Dishes", page 34
pinchos see "Gastronomic Terms", page 55
pincho moruno see "National Dishes", page 34
piñones pine nuts
piscina swimming pool
pistachos pistachio nuts
pisto manchego see "Regional Dishes", page 44
placer to please
plátano banana
plato dish; course; plate
plato, al see "Gastronomic Terms", page 54
plato combinado see "Gastronomic Terms", page 55
plaza square

pochas a la Navarra see "Regional Dishes", page 50

poco little; not much; a few

poder to be able, can

pollo chicken; **pollo al chilindrón** see "Regional Dishes", page 50; **pollo al Jerez** see "Regional Dishes", page 38; **pollo asado** see "National Dishes", page 35; **pollo campurriano** see "Regional Dishes", page 40

polo popsicle

polvorones see "Sweets, Cakes, and Pastries", page 21

polvos de talco talcum powder

pomelo grapefruit

poner to put; to place

poner la mesa to lay the table

por for; per

porción portion

porque why; because

posible possible

postal postcard

postre dessert

precio price

preferir to prefer

preguntar question

preparar to prepare

prisa hurry; haste

probar to taste

propina tip

propio just; really; own

puchero canario see "Regional Dishes", page 42

pueblo country; village; people

puerros leeks

puerta door

pulpa pulp; flesh

pulpo octopus; **pulpo afeira** see "Regional Dishes", page 47; **pulpo a la gallega**, see "National Dishes", page 35

puntas honey mushrooms

puré purée, see "The Basics", page 27

puro cigar

purrusalda see "Regional Dishes", page 49

puzol see "Cheeses", page 11

que that

¡qué aproveche! Have a good meal!

quedar/se to stay; to remain; to be left

quemado burnt

quemar to burn
querer to want
queso cheese
queso de los Beyos see "Cheeses", page 11
quesucos de Lebeña see "Cheeses", page 11
quien who
quitar to remove
quitar la monda to peel; **quitar la grasa** to scour; to remove the grease from; **quitar la cáscara** to shell
quizás perhaps

rábanos radishes
ración portion
radio radio
rallado grated
rape angler fish, goosefish, monkfish; **rape a la gallega** see "Regional Dishes", page 47
rápidamente quickly
rápido rapid; quick; fast
rebado de Cáceres see "Regional Dishes", page 44
recao de Binéfar see "Regional Dishes", page 50
receta recipe
recibir to receive
recibo receipt

reclamación complaint
reembolso refund
región region
regresar to return
regreso return
reloj watch, clock
relleno stuffing; filling; stuffed; filled, see "Gastronomic Terms", page 55
remolacha beetroot; beet
reo con almejas sea trout and clams, see "Regional Dishes", page 47
repollo cabbage
reservado reserved; booked
reservar to reserve; to book
responder to reply; to answer; to respond
restaurante restaurant
resto change
retraso delay
retraso, con late
revuelto see "Gastronomic Terms", page 56; **revuelto de gambas y ajetes** see "National Dishes", page 35
Ribeiro see "Wines", page 24
riñón kidney
riñones al Jerez see "Regional Dishes", page 38

róbalo grey mullet

rodajas, en see "Gastronomic Terms", page 55

rojo red

rollos roulades, see "The Basics" page 27

rollos de ternera veal roulades, see "National Dishes", page 35

romero rosemary

romper to break

Rosal see "Wines", page 24

rosca/ón or **rosquilla** ring-shaped cake; donut

roto broken

Rueda see "Wines", page 24

ruido noise

ruidoso noisy

rústico country-style

sábado Saturday

saber to know

sabor flavor; taste

saborear to taste; to enjoy; to season

sabroso tasty

sal salt

sala hall; lounge; room

salado salty; salted; savory

salar to salt; to add salt to

salchicha sausage, see "Cold Cut Meats", page 16

salchichón see "Cold Cut Meats", page 16

salero salt-cellar

salida exit

salir to go out; to come out; to leave

salmón salmon; **salmón ahumado** smoked salmon; **salmón a noso estilo** see "Regional Dishes", page 47; **salmón asado** baked salmon, see "National Dishes", page 35

salmonetes red mullet

salpicón de Murcia see "Regional Dishes", page 52

salsa sauce; **salsa tártara** see "Gastronomic Terms", page 55; **salsa verde** see "Gastronomic Terms", page 55

salvia sage

sancocho canario see "Regional Dishes", page 42

sandía water-melon

sangría see "Other Specialties", page 25

San Simón see "Cheeses", page 11

sardinas sardines; **sardinas fritas** fried sardines, see "National Dishes", page 35

sartén frying pan; saucepan

seco dry

sed thirst

según/do second

sello stamp

semana week

señora lady; madam; Mrs

señorita young woman; Miss

separado separate

sepias cuttlefish

septiembre September

servicio service; service charge

servilleta serviette; napkin

sesos brains

setas mushrooms

sidra see "Other Specialties", page 25

siempre always; ever

silla chair

silla para bebés high chair

simple simple

sin without

sin alcohol non-alcoholic; alcohol-free

sitio place; position; job; seat

sobrasada see "Cold Cut Meats", page 16

sobre envelope

sofrito onion and herbs browned in oil

soja soya

solo alone

sólo only

solomillo see "National Dishes", page 35

sombrero hat; sombrero

sopa soup; **sopa castellana** see "Regional Dishes", page 43; **sopa del Teide** see "Regional Dishes", page 42; **sopa de puré** see "National Dishes", page 35; **sopas de ajo** see "National Dishes", page 35; **sopa seca mallorquina** see "Regional Dishes", page 41

sorbete sorbet; sherbet **sorbete de naranja** see "National Dishes", page 35

soria see "Cheeses", page 11

subir to go up; to climb; to mount; to get on; to raise

suceder to happen; to take place; to occur

sucio dirty

suflé de patatas see "National Dishes", page 36

suido pork; pig

Suiza Switzerland

suquet de peix see "Regional Dishes", page 45

sur south

sutil thin; fine; subtle

tacita coffee cup

también also

tapa lid

tapas snack

tapón cork; stopper; cap

tarde evening; late

tarjeta de crédito credit card

tarrina tureen

tarta tart; pie; cake **tarta de plátanos** see "Regional Dishes", page 42

tasca tavern; inn

taza cup

té tea

teléfono telephone

temperatura temperature

tenedor fork

tener to have; to hold; to keep

tener que to have to

tentempié appetizer

terminar to finish; to end

ternero veal

terraza terrace

tetilla see "Cheeses", page 11

tiempo weather; time

tiempo, del room temperature

tienda shop

tinta, en su see "Gastronomic Terms", page 55

tirar to throw away

tirita Band Aid

tisana herb tea

toalla towel

tocinillos see "Sweets, Cakes, and Pastries", page 22

tocino lard

todavía more; still; nevertheless

todo all; everything

tombet de peix see "Regional Dishes", page 41

tomillo thyme

Toro see "Wines", page 24

torrijas see "Sweets, Cakes, and Pastries", page 22

torta, see "Other Specialties", page 26

torta con mermelada jam tart

torteta see "Cold Cut Meats", page 16

tortilla omelette; **tortilla de ropa vieja** see "National

Dishes", page 36; **tortilla española** see "National Dishes", page 36 and "Recipes", page 65; **tortilla francesa** see "National Dishes", page 36; **tortilla paisana** see "National Dishes", page 36

tostado toasted

trabajar to work

trabajo work

traer to carry; to bring

tranquilo quiet; calm

tren train

triturado minced; chopped

triturar to mince; to chop

trucha trout; **truchas a la Navarra** see "Regional Dishes", page 50; **truchas al horno** baked trout, see "National Dishes", page 36; **truchas escabechadas** see "National Dishes", page 36

Turín Turin

txangurro relleno see "National Dishes", page 49

último last

ulloa see "Cheeses", page 11

untado greasy; oily

usar to use

uvas grapes

uvas pasas raisins

vacaciones holidays, vacation

vacío empty

vainilla vanilla

Valdeorras see "Wines", page 24

valdeteja see "Cheeses", page 12

Valdevimbre see "Wines", page 24

vapor, al see "Gastronomic Terms", page 54

vaso glass

vegetariano vegetarian see "Gastronomic Terms", page 56

vela candle

vender to sell

venir to come

ventana window

ver to see

veraniego summer (adj.)

verano summer

verde green

verdura vegetable

vieira see "Seafood", page 19

vieiras con col see "Regional Dishes", page 47

viejo old

viernes Friday

villalón see "Cheeses", page 12

vinagre vinegar

vinagreta, a la see see "Gastronomic Terms", page 54

vino wine; **v. blanco** white wine; **v. fuerte** full-bodied wine; **v. ligero** light wine; **v. rosado** rosé; **v. tinto** red wine

vista sight, view

vitaminas vitamins

volver to return; to go back; to come back

vuelo flight

vuelta tour; turn; trip; revolution

yema (huevo) egg yolk

yemas see "Sweets, Cakes, and Pastries", page 22

yoghurt yoghurt

zanahoria carrot

zumo juice

zumo natural freshly-squeezed fruit juice

INDEX